INNER REVIVAL

KEVIN EATON

REAL HOPE BOOKS

CONTENTS

Dedication	v
Preface	vii
1. You Can Live Again	1
2. Never Give Up, Never Give In	11
3. Fanning the Flame	21
4. Time Alone	31
5. Go Time	39
6. Bloom and Boom Where You Are Planted	47
7. The Power is Essential – The Power of the Holy Spirit	53
8. Humility is Essential	59
9. Rise Up and Step Up	65
10. The Big 3 + 1	71
11. Serve God Completely	81
12. Actively Resist	91
13. The Greatest Virtue	95
14. Finish Well	105

DEDICATION

Dedication To my Family: My Dad taught me humility, worked hard and tried to bring out the best in people. My Mom taught me to laugh at myself, to not take myself so seriously, to do the right thing, and be a balanced person. To my Step Mom and Step Dad who went out of their way to be there for me and to accept me. My sister showed me not to pay more attention to obstacles than needed, not to focus on the bad, but on the good and fun times. My brother also taught me not to take mistakes so seriously, but to enjoy life and people, and to be adventurous. My wife shows me how to show hospitality and to take time to make a difference in the lives of others. My son, Michael showed me how to stay on task and not give up and to humbly serve others. My son, Luke taught me how to be diligent and finish what you start and to do it with excellence. My son, Joshua showed me the importance of being yourself and not worrying about what others think, and to forgive people and move on. To My Uncle Levell, who spent time with me and was an example to me when I was a troubled teen. He never judged me, but created opportunities for me to prosper. To friends throughout my life who have all been so unique, encouraging and challenging. To Josh Bennett, who encouraged me to finish this and always asked "How is the book coming?" To my Pastors that I have sat under, who sacrificed their lives to share the Good News and took time to make an impact on my life. To Pastor Greg Laurie, for being the example of someone who does what God equipped him to do, who inspired me to be alive and active in my faith, through growing up, listening to his messages and reading his book, *Lost Boy*, which I recommend everyone read.

Of course, I dedicate this book to the Lord Jesus, who saved me and sanctified me through His blood, who always loves me and encourages me to keep trusting and following Him, and ensures me that there is a heaven and how joyful it will be with him for eternity. He gave me Life and promises it is more than this short life on earth

This book is also dedicated to those who will read it, and attempt or succeed to practice the principles in it, which are disciplines found in the Bible. And to those who have been plugging along and believe, but don't feel they are getting anywhere. They don't have the intensity they once had, or they never had it at all, but they know there is more and desire it, even if they are discouraged now. They hope that they can be revived and stay revived. This book is to tell them: Your faith can be revived; your life can be on fire. You can fulfill your destiny on this earth. You can be alive again and strong in God and stay that way. It's never too late for you!

PREFACE

This book was inspired by a sermon I gave on personal revival at a small home church setting to a few people. The message was called "How to Change the world." The premise is this: If we want to see the world changed and see God glorified and see true Revival, we need to start with ourselves and be personally revived. We must maintain this inner revival. The person must first be changed before any good change can happen in this world.

It was just after the passing of my Grandmother, when I was really feeling that I was not living my life to the potential God wanted me to. I was praying for direction and specifically praying for an answer to what God had for me; what was His specific will for me at this time in my life? Somehow, I felt He was telling me to write a book. He dropped all the chapters in my mind and laid out the outline, and so I believe he wanted me to write this book. Since I feel he has called me to write this and that He placed all the chapters in my mind so easily, I need to be obedient and finish this. That's why I wrote this, and every time I pray as to what God wants me to do, this book sticks in my mind as a first priority. This has been tougher than I thought, being my first book. The toughest thing is to sit down and to be disciplined to take the time and fill in the chapters. I could find many things I wanted to do besides this,

Preface

but I believe so strongly it is His will for me. So here it is, an act of obedience as to what I believe the Lord put on my heart and mind to write.

This is by no means a self-help book, or a book about how to accomplish great things by self-accomplishment, but in a relationship with God, there are choices and actions we must take to allow God to work in us. These choices and actions should always be done in faith, not out of duty. They should center on and around obedience, out of a love and a desire to please our maker. Each chapter in this book brings a different, important biblical principal or practice that we can choose to do, which I believe will help keep us revived, so that when God brings a true revival, we are ready to fulfill the role that He has for us. That's what this book is about: how to be revived and how to maintain revival, so that we can be used to help others come alive and stay alive.

The main purpose of this book is to encourage you in your walk with God to be all he has called you to be and to help you accomplish His will in your life. God's word tells us to encourage each other in these verses Hebrews 3:13; 1 Thessalonians 5:11 NIV, and to consider how to *"spur one another on toward love and good deeds,"* in Hebrews 10:24. This is one of the gifts I believe God has given me. I hope that in spite of me, God will use this book to encourage you to be revived. The teacher always learns more than the student, so I am the one who will benefit the most from writing this; that's just the way it works. Being my first book, it is an act of obedience to what I believe God wants me to do, but more than that, it is a learning experience, an encouragement and reminder to live this life to the fullest for God, for myself, and I hope, for the readers.

I believe this book may serve as a catalyst to get you going, and I hope it does.

So, I want to be obedient and write this book to get you ignited, so your life can explode for God. There is nothing better than to be revived and to be truly alive and on fire for God. I hope and pray that this happens for you as you read this book and continue to pursue God.

This book is also for those who feel there is something missing in their lives, for those that feel there should be something more, or feel

Preface

that there is no hope for them anymore. For the Christian that has lost hope and for the Non-Christian who has no real hope. It is for the person that is down and needs a little boost. All of us need some encouragement sometimes, or something that will get us back on track. Too many people live and die without accomplishing what they were intended for. I don't wish that on anyone. So that is one reason I am so passionate about writing on this topic. He knows I need inner revival, and so do a lot of other people like me.

My prayer and goal is that you will use this one life you have been given to fulfill it in the way God intended you to; that His life will flow through you in a powerful, dynamic, and wonderful way. I hope that this book will be used as a poker to stoke the coals burning in you, so that you will be on fire for Him, and that you will thrive in the relationship God created you for in the first place- to walk with Him.

1

YOU CAN LIVE AGAIN

Before there is a Revival in the world, there has to be an inner revival. Christians around the world pray for revival all the time. Revival is bringing something back to life. People want revival in the economy and in politics but are not always willing to get involved in the change. Neither is the person who wants a change in their life or expects God to move in their life. Revival is known to be a divine intervention that causes change and brings life back to a cause, to make it important again. Some refer to revival as a Move of God.

In 1982, I attended a large Jesus Festival called Jesus West Coast. Besides hearing the late, great Keith Green speak and play music, there were many other great speakers. I still have some of the notes from that conference, except for one evangelist named Mario Murillo. I was so intrigued with his fire and passion that I couldn't write any notes, I just had to pay attention. He talked about revival, and I remember the essence of what he was saying. It was something like this: "Instead of waiting for a Move of God, have a Move of God!" If we want God to revive us and our world, then have a Move of God! He was saying it was up to us, not God. God always wants to move on the behalf of men, but we need to let Him move through us, and the time is now. He has given us free will; God is waiting for us to respond, move and act. We, of course, can do nothing without God's working, but He is always looking for us to move to act in faith.

I will always remember those words that Mario said and believe it is true. If we want God to move, then there is something we need to do. Faith is an action. We can sit around and wait for revival forever, but unless we respond with an action, nothing will happen. We have to allow God to change us, to revive us, to move in us, if we want to see Him move. God is the initiator, the power, the enabler, but he doesn't force us to respond. It takes an act of faith and obedience on our part in the relationship, then we can sit back and watch Him work.

Are you ready for revival? A Personal Revival? Do you want to see God move in your life? Then do something to make it happen. Read His word, pray to Him, obey Him. Do what it takes to come back to life again. Finish this book, and act and live out the principles in it.

Like myself, I am sure there are times you feel revived and other times you don't. When going through trials and hardships, it seems harder to see God moving. I do believe you can come to a place where you can experience revival in the hard times. In some of our lowest times in life is where God shines the strongest, teaches us the greatest lessons, does the greatest miracles, if we let Him.

I remember a time, not long ago, when I felt I had lost my influence, that my life was not really mattering, and that I had failed God in what he put me on Earth for; I had lost my saltiness. I am referring to the passage in Matthew 5:13, where Jesus said *"You are the salt of the earth. But if the salt loses its saltiness, how can it be made salty again? It is no longer good for anything, except to be thrown out and trampled underfoot."* I was feeling condemned and was asking God how salt could be made salty again to make it useful. I was thinking there was no answer, that my life was no longer useful, and that it was only to be thrown out according to that verse. God dropped the answer to me in the form of a song, I picked up my guitar and wrote a song called "Salty Again." The main line in the song was God saying to me "I will make you salty again, if you come to me." Just like when Jesus told his disciples in Matthew 19:23-24 *"I tell you the truth, it is hard for a rich man to enter the kingdom of heaven. Again I tell you, it is easier for a camel to go through the eye of a needle than for a rich man to enter the kingdom of God."* Next they asked *"Who then can be saved?"* I love Jesus' response. He looked at them and said, *"With man, this is impossible, but with God, all things are possible."* None of us are too far gone, too used up for God to save us. There is always hope with God.

Nothing is impossible for You, so don't ever let the devil make you feel that way. God is able to revive you, just as he was able to revive me. He is in the business of reviving; he is an expert at bringing things back to life. Ask Him to do it, and He will!

Dry Bones Again?

The famous passage of scripture used for many revival messages is found in the book of Ezekiel, chapter 37. The prophet is taken by the Spirit of the Lord to a valley full of bones that were very dry. The bones represented Israel, and they said that their bones were dry and their hope was gone. The Lord asked Ezekiel if he thought the bones could live again. The prophet answered *"You alone know."* God then told him to do something that caused the bones to come alive. He told him to prophesy, to speak God's word to them. We must go to God alone for the answers, only he knows. He will tell us what to do, what we must do, if we want to see His will be done and life come to our dry bones again. You can live again. There is hope for you, no matter what you have gone through or are going through now. God loves you and will breathe life into your dry bones if you allow him and follow him. You may feel like a skeleton, with nothing left of life, but I guarantee, God can make you alive again, just like he did then; just like He has done for Israel; just like He has done many times. Read Ezekiel 37 and speak what God said there. *"You will live."* Your hope will be restored!

Our Responsibility

Do we have a part to play when it comes to revival? Really, I am asking you. In the great Moves of God in history, did the people who were involved and instrumental in the move just sit back and expect God to do everything? In the Ezekiel account, he did his part; he prophesied and did what God told him. He obeyed and acted. The early church obeyed and acted. All the great revivals that have occurred in history, like the Great Awakenings, the Azusa Street Revival, the Jesus Movement, great crusades where Billy Graham led millions to Christ, happened because people obeyed and acted. They gave effort.

Self-Effort or Do I Expect God to Do It All?

When we hear the term self-effort, we think that we are talking about living and accomplishing everything by our own strength and efforts. We are not talking about that because we all know that nothing that we have done caused God to save us or call us. Read 2 Timothy 1:8-10. God is the initiator; He has accomplished it all, and He calls us to walk in faith and obedience to what He has called us to. He is the one that led Ezekiel to the valley and told him what to do. In our relationship with Him, He expects us to give our effort, our all, to His purposes. King David fought battles but knew the victory came from the Lord. He also knew he had to give effort; he had to obey in faith to win the battles.

In Philippians 2:12, we are told to "*Work out our salvation with fear and trembling.*" God does expect us to "work out" what He has given us. He really wants us to give our all, our best effort, not a half-hearted response. We are not to be self-reliant, but God reliant, knowing He will bring about the best result.

What Does This Have to Do with Revival?

We all have times of weakness, failures, and attacks from the devil. I have had times where I thought everyone and everything was against me. I later realized that it was an attack of Satan to defeat me, or he used the situation or people to tempt me to act wrongly and disobey. Too many times, we struggle or give up because we fail to continue to give effort, when we should be having faith in God. Going through hard times, trials and temptations is where most of us get confused and don't act as we should through the situation. Hopefully, we learn through them, before we make too many mistakes. those times are where our faith is really perfected, and we learn valuable lessons. I believe an inner revival happens when we learn how to fight, in these times of death and despair in our lives, and learn to choose life the next time it happens. That is called spiritual growth. When we learn to trust God in the hardest times in our lives. We will talk more about this in chapter 12. If we truly want to live a life revived, then we must know that a life of faith takes action and obedience.

There Is a Process to Revival

Look at what Ezekiel did. He was a priest to the Jews who had been driven from their land and were in exile in a land that was not theirs. Their hope in God had been dashed, but it was all caused by their rebellion against God. God was punishing the Jews and had called Ezekiel to speak to them on His behalf as a Prophet. God told Ezekiel to speak to the Israelites, whether they listened or not. He told Ezekiel not to rebel like Israel had. Ezekiel listened to God. He did not rebel against Him, but obeyed and did what God said. Ezekiel kept at the process of obeying God. He did not let the rebellion of his own people dissuade him. He kept on doing God's will. He was a priest first, before God called Him to be his mouth piece. He was in the place God wanted Him to be, and God used Him to tell of the restoration of Jerusalem. He let God show him; he paid attention to God, and he obeyed God.

If you have done as Ezekiel, you have listened to God, and let Him show you that if you pay attention, if you obey what God says, then He will come into your life and revive you. Maybe you have not let God show you. Maybe you have not paid attention to God or have not been obedient, like most of us and the Jews at that time. There is always hope. God never changes, just as those dry bones came to life when Ezekiel prophesied, so God's people can be made alive again. God loves you as He loves His people, Israel, and He had a purpose to restore them and save the world.

The whole Bible tells God's plan to save mankind. He wants to restore you. No matter what you have been through, no matter how you have failed God, he made the way for you. He made the sacrifice of His Son for you. You need to get into the process by believing it. Then you will be able to listen to God, to pay attention to God, and obey God, just like Ezekiel did.

Before You Move On

If you are a Christian, I want you to stop for a minute, and tell the Lord that you want to be revived, that you want more. Ask Him to move in your life, to make the dead areas alive again, to raise you up to do His will. Make a commitment, right now, to follow Him, no matter the cost. Start obeying what He tells you to do. If you are not willing to do that, then you should just put this book down now. Without His spirit and His breath of life in you, you cannot really do much. You have to be full of Him to be fruitful. You have to be so attached to Him so that you are a branch, connected to Him who is the vine from which all life comes from. (see John 15:5) You will continue to wither, if you do not seek Him and depend on Him for everything.

Easy to say, I know, but you must do it. Let his fire burn out whatever is not of Him and blaze through your life afresh. Then you can fulfill the purpose and plan He has for you. Go ahead and do it. I will wait. I dare you to give everything to Him.

Stop Here.

If you are not a Christian, I also want you to stop here. The rest of the book really won't make sense, if you don't stop here and make this choice. Pay careful attention to this section. Accepting Christ into your life will be the best choice you can ever make in this life. Just ask someone who has been changed by Him. This is the most important section in this book for you. I want to give you a moment here to think about Jesus, who went to the cross, to die for your sins, and rose again, conquering death.

He said in John 14:6, *"I am the way and the truth and the life. No one comes to the Father except through me."* And in 1 John 5:12 the Bible tells us, *"Whoever has the Son has life; whoever does not have the Son of God does not have life."*

There is no other way to find true life, to find eternal life. You either have it, or you don't. Ephesians 2:8 says *"For it is by grace you have been saved, through faith—and this is not from yourselves, it is the gift of God—"*

You can continue in this life, masquerading that you have it all together, but there is only one Savior and way to God, heaven and eternal life. You have to take the step of faith, and ask Him to forgive you of your sins, to make Him your Lord. You need to take this opportunity, and do it now. Ask Jesus to save you today. Accept the free gift of life now.

I made that choice years ago and have never regretted it. I prayed to God and asked Him, "If You are real, show me. Come into my life, forgive me, take the sin out of my life." He answered. He did. You won't ever know, until you take a step to trust Him. If you say a prayer like I did, I am positive you will never regret that choice.

So, please, don't put it off. It's time to make a commitment. Time to stop playing and to get real. A lot of people believe in God in their minds, on their terms, with their ideas. It's time to give it all to God, and let Him be your Savior. Please, take a moment, and ask Jesus to be the Lord of your life now, and start following Him.

The rest of this book is about choices you can make that will bring you to a place of personal revival, choices that will leave you "Stoked." I first heard that word "Stoked" when I lived at Newport Beach, California for a short time in the late 70's. It was surfer lingo, that was used when someone was really excited, like by catching a great wave or by getting high from a good drug. But it was only used when one word could describe something super awesome, something that stirred you up, that amazed you beyond belief. No other words could describe it—you were just "stoked." A few months later, when I accepted Christ into my life I was "stoked," and I continue to be "stoked" by what God can do. I was going to title this book *Stoked*, but someone already used that, and my experience in Christ has come to mean more to me than one word. Knowing Jesus is happiness and more! It's better than just being stoked or excited. It's not a onetime experience. He keeps changing you, keeps saving you; He keeps making you more alive.

Convinced

Something else before you can go on, that will help you throughout your life, is to make a signpost. Write down the date that you put your faith in Christ so that you can come back to that when you are tempted to doubt. You have to know that you know, that you know. The Apostle Paul talked about being thoroughly convinced. You don't have to know everything in one day, but this date can be a reminder to go back to, like a monument set in stone. Make a statement of your faith, and write down the date that you have made a commitment to Christ. The devil will assuredly try to make you forget this day and make you doubt your decision. Surely, you will have doubts, and you will be ever learning, but you need to get that assurance within you. You have to be fully convinced at some point. So, if you have prayed and asked Jesus to save you today, write this date down and keep it. Everything before this date is B.C.

Here are some verses from the Bible on assurance before you move on.

> *"For Christ's love compels us, because we are convinced that one died for all, and therefore all died." 2 Corinthians 5:14*

> *"That is why I am suffering as I am. Yet this is no cause for shame, because I know whom I have believed, and am convinced that he is able to guard what I have entrusted to him until that day." 2 Timothy 1:12*

> *"Now faith is confidence in what we hope for and assurance about what we do not see." Hebrews 11:1*

"Whoever believes in the Son of God accepts this testimony. Whoever does not believe God has made him out to be a liar, because they have not believed the testimony God has given about his Son. And this is the testimony: God has given us eternal life, and this life is in his Son. Whoever has the Son has life; whoever does not have the Son of God does not have life." 1 John 5:10-13

You can be assured that God loves you and that he wants you to be strong in your faith. He wants to revive you, if you are feeling dead. He wants to keep you thriving with His abundant life, so that you can fulfill His purposes for you and others on this earth. So, commit yourself to personal revival, and let the dry bones live!

2

NEVER GIVE UP, NEVER GIVE IN

I was planning on starting to write this chapter tomorrow, but I believe God reminded me of something, and I needed to write while it was fresh on my mind. So, it is 12:29am, and I need to get this typed out.

Not long after becoming a Christian, I will never forget this one night... I had been a Christian for several months and was beginning an awesome journey of faith that was very exciting to me. I was home alone in the little house the Church owned, where I had become a part-time janitor and a full-time student of the Bible. It was late at night, and I got down on the floor. I think I was trying to pray, but I felt this presence telling me to give up. I must have had some doubts as to if this relationship with God was real. Was I just being fooled? I wasn't really doubting myself, but I felt it was Satan and demons trying to get me to quit. I remember getting on my hands and knees, and it literally felt like a slew of demons had jumped on my back. I felt trapped and like they were pressing me to give in, almost trying to force me to give in. I could not call out for help to my Christian neighbors next door, for I could hardly speak, the pressure was so strong. I was trying to pray to God and felt the pressure to give in strengthen, like they were trying to pin me and kill me, or at least kill my spiritual life that I had found. I then thought of a last-ditch effort. I would read the word of God. The weight of the oppression was so strong, I had to crawl with all my strength to my Bible. I opened it and started reading. The demons left instantly! The pressure left instantly. I then fell asleep in peace and safety. Never again did I feel Satan or his demons trying that trick on me. Satan made the mistake of letting me find out that if I resisted him, he had to flee. He has never tried that stunt on me again, and through that experience, I vowed that I will never up on God, and I will never give in to Satan or his demons or lying voices.

Aware of His Schemes

Shortly after that, I had what I would call a spiritual dream. I have not had too many of those dreams in my life, but this one stood out among all dreams I have had. The reason it stands out is that I was awakened by pain in my back. Not just a normal back pain, but they were fiery little knives hitting my flesh and sinking in. The dream was like you see in a movie. I was walking down a street, and I felt someone following me. I heard footsteps behind me. I sped up, and the steps behind me sped up on the sidewalk. I kept going faster, down alleyways and streets, but the steps were now running after me as I was running. I went into a building to hide, but the steps kept getting closer. I tried to lose this stranger that was following me, but it seemed he was gaining on me with every attempt I made to hide. I ran to the end of a hallway, to an elevator, to escape, but the elevator didn't work. I knew this dark figure was behind me. I looked at him. He was wearing all black, with shiny, black, pointed shoes. In his hand was what looked like a painter's palette, with colored paints on it. The palette began spinning in his hand. I knew I was in trouble. I looked for a way to defend myself. If only I had a gun or a knife. I was reaching all over my body, but I had nothing; I was defenseless. The spinning palette started shooting little knives off of it, right toward me. They were like little miniature knives that were on fire. All I could do was turn my back for protection. The knives started hitting me in the back, and I could feel each one hit me in the flesh and stick in. The pain was so real. The palette just kept spinning, and the knives kept coming. I could do nothing. The pain was getting so bad, I thought I would probably die from the wounds. My body winced as they hit me. Then I woke up as they were hitting me. The pain actually woke me up. I literally felt the pain. Fortunately, it was only a dream; there were no knives sticking in my back. I thought about that dream a lot, and I realized what I was lacking was a shield... the shield of faith the Bible talks about in Ephesians 6:16, to defend myself.

The reason I am writing about these experiences is because they were real to me, and they showed me that the devil is out to make us give up or just hurt or kill us. He will, if we let him. I have known of too many people that heard voices telling them to give in, to end it all, that there was no hope. Some were friends or relatives who ended up committing suicide. I want the readers of this book to be aware of Satan's schemes. Jesus said in John 10:10, *"The thief comes only to steal and kill and destroy; I have come that they may have life, and have it to the full."* And this in John 8:44; *"He was a murderer from the beginning, not holding to the truth, for there is no truth in him. When he lies, he speaks his native language, for he is a liar and the father of lies."* It is plain Satan is a liar and a murderer. He can be subtle or outright bold. In the beginning, he got Eve to question God's command, and then he outright lied. He pulls no punches; neither should you. Never, never, never, give in to a lie or one of his schemes. Anything that is a lie is from Satan. Truth is from God. If you are starting to question things that you know are the truth, then you should be aware, because a lie is coming. Don't give in. That's how people get into cults, by questioning the truth. The next thing they do is believe a lie.

More Aware of the Promises

Once Satan knows you won't fall for an obvious lie, he will try something more subtle, maybe some condemnation to make you give up. Well, this book is about how to not fall for those tricks that can bring you down, those tricks that make you want to give up or believe a lie. You can start by not giving up, no matter how you feel, or if you have become confused. You need to focus on what God has said, His clear promises that are recorded in the Bible. God has general promises to everyone, and He also speaks personal and specific ones to us. The personal calls and promises should line up with His Word. That's an easy way to know if they are lies or not. If they line up with the truth of God's word, you can generally bank on them and leave the timing up to God. Don't dismiss them and forget them, but instead, act on faith to do what God wants you to do. Be more aware of the promises God has made. Never give up on His promises—they are the truth. Here are just five of the thousands of promises found in God's word:

"Be strong and courageous. Do not be afraid or terrified because of them, for the Lord your God goes with you; He will never leave you nor forsake you." Deuteronomy 31:6

"So do not fear, for I am with you; do not be dismayed, for I am your God. I will strengthen you and help you; I will uphold you with my righteous right hand." Isaiah 41:10

"For God so loved the world that He gave His one and only Son, that whoever believes in Him shall not perish but have eternal life." John 3:16

"Here I am! I stand at the door and knock. If anyone hears my voice and opens the door, I will come in and eat with that person, and they with me." Revelation 3:20

"But they that wait upon the Lord shall renew their strength; they shall mount up with wings as eagles; they shall run, and not be weary; and they shall walk, and not faint." Isaiah 40:31

Lose a Turn

Sometimes you have to wait, move in another direction, or learn something before you move on, but you should never give up. You might have acted on what you thought was God's will, and it doesn't work out. You have invested a lot of time in a direction you thought God was calling you, and it ends abruptly. Sometimes God closes doors to protect us or to cause us to grow in another area, but it's always for our good. God doesn't stop calling you. He may have accomplished his purpose for you as you stepped out in faith, and he may have something bigger for you.

Something bigger isn't always what we think it is. Doors sometimes stay closed for years; some doors never open when we think they should.

There is a famous pastor who travels the world doing marriage conferences. He wanted to be in ministry as a pastor, but the door never opened. He was getting older and thought he would never become a pastor, so he started doing marriage conferences which became very successful. The pastor in his church left, and the elders asked him to be the pastor when he was in his 50's. He has now grown and expanded that church to several campuses and a school. He thought it was too late for him, but God used him even more than he expected, and he still does the conferences.

God wants us to be obedient and dependent on Him. If we take one of His promises and try to make ourselves God, He will end it, (I am saying by our own efforts and our own strength, instead of trusting God.) There are things I thought God was calling me to do, so I stepped out in faith. Things didn't go the way I dreamed they would, and I had to stop, but I learned that God is in control. He was teaching me things that would help me later and caused me to grow, and used those times to prepare me for something bigger. The something bigger is probably not what we had expected, and it may even involve us giving up on our dreams to be obedient to God and His dreams for us. God's plans for us are always better than our own, but we need to always stay active in living out that calling God has for us. To do that as we have said before: You have to listen, you have to obey, you have to pursue and follow Him alone, and do what He wants you to do.

When things don't go the way that we want them to, that doesn't mean we should give up, and these situations should not cause us to give up on God. Just like playing a board game when you were young and you hit the space that says Lose a Turn, it is no fun. Sometimes we need to lose a turn; it gives us time to strategize and to seek God more for what He has called us to do. We will finish the game, but we don't need to be first. We cannot expect to live a revived life if we quit. Many people "check out" from living a revived life; they are content with where they are or have no hope of being alive because of setbacks, heartache and disappointments. Losing a turn is no reason to quit. Feeling like a loser is no reason to quit. When it looks like you are losing in the game of life, hang in there; your turn is coming again; God has not forgotten you. If you can hold on, even if it is by an invisible thread, you will be happy that you persevered and stayed in a position to take your turn.

Faith Takes Perseverance
A Revived Life Takes Perseverance, Not Giving In or Up.

Personally, I have seen my prayers answered that took years. One of them took 27 years to see God's hand move in a family relationship. So, we should never give up in praying for family, friends, and others.

People have been healed who I thought would surely die. A Christian I had worked with who had liver failure and was in a comma; he was waiting for months and months for a liver, and he was close to death. When he came out of a coma, they released him to go home, still in very critical condition. But on the way home from the hospital, they called him back because a liver came in. That guy is still alive and doing well.

Pastor Lance, who was the music pastor at the church we attended had told the congregation about his son when playing, had fallen and hit his head on a rock. He then suffered a stroke and was partially paralyzed. While in the hospital, he felt like giving up, but something finally came over him. He was resolved not to give up on his son's restoration. There was not a dry eye in the church that day, when his son came running across the stage, able to run and play again.

We all know that not every prayer is answered the way we want, and many times we don't understand why a loved one passes away while another one is healed. Just because we don't understand God's purposes in these situations, His omniscient wisdom and plans fully; it gives us no right to give up. Instead, we need to press on and be persistent in our trust. It is easy to find excuses to not pursue God and not trust Him completely. Be persistent in doing what is right, not just when things are going your way. The great story of Joseph in the Bible found in Genesis chapters 37-47

Joseph gives us a clear example of what can happen in one's life who doesn't give up. He was thrown in a pit, sold as a slave by brothers, lied about, framed, thrown in prison, forgotten, but finally God's promise came true. He came to be the man in charge who ended up saving his family and restoring them. God can take you from what seems to be a hopeless situation and put you in the highest position in the land if he wants to. God will bless you and use you for his glory if you remain faithful and do not give up. Maybe you have been in a pit, been lied about and hurt by others. Don't give up because of other people, and don't give up if you have failed God in the past. Now is the time to turn around, to get your attitude aligned with God, who never gives up on you. God is your biggest fan. He knows how great it will be when you reach the finish line. He is waiting for you, don't give up.

"Blessed is the one who perseveres under trial because, having stood the test, that person will receive the crown of life that the Lord has promised to those who love Him." James 1:12

Something Is Said About Diligence

"For this very reason, make every effort to add to your faith, goodness; and to goodness, knowledge; and to knowledge, self-control; and to self-control, perseverance; and to perseverance, godliness; and to godliness, mutual affection; and to mutual affection, love. For if you possess these qualities in increasing measure, they will keep you from being ineffective and unproductive in your knowledge of our Lord Jesus Christ. But whoever does not have them is nearsighted and blind, forgetting that they have been cleansed from their past sins. Therefore, my brothers and sisters, make every effort to confirm your calling and election. For if you do these things, you will never stumble, and you will receive a rich welcome into the eternal kingdom of our Lord and Savior Jesus Christ." 2 Peter 1:5-11

Notice in the above passages that Peter tells us to "*make every effort*" to add to our faith several things, one of them being perseverance. In the original Greek language, perseverance means to have a cheerful (or hopeful) endurance, consistency, patient continuance.

Anything that is worth anything takes work. Working on this book was very difficult for me. It was not easy for me to sit down and study and write. I could think of a lot of other things that I would rather do. A pastor I once had often reminded us that people today love to start things, but don't like to finish them. I have settled in my mind that I will not start any other project until this one is done—I have slacked off long enough. I am easily distracted by other ideas and projects. In fact, I have been tempted to work on the business I want to start, but every time I do, it just slows down the progress of this book, so I am trying to stick to this until it is done, which is very difficult for me, more difficult than I expected when I had the idea for the book. It takes perseverance to finish something. I am slowly finding this out. You have to finish what God wants you to finish. I believe there is a great reward in finishing. I know that I am including a lot of scripture in this book, but I have to include these verses that I think help sum up this topic and give us encouragement about persevering. So here they are:

> *Then Jesus told his disciples a parable to show them that they should always pray and not give up. He said: "In a certain town, there was a judge who neither feared God nor cared what people thought. And there was a widow in that town who kept coming to him with the plea, 'Grant me justice against my adversary.' "For some time, he refused. But finally, he said to himself, 'Even though I don't fear God or care what people think, yet because this widow keeps bothering me, I will see that she gets justice, so that she won't eventually come and attack me!'" And the Lord said, "Listen to what the unjust judge says. And will not God bring about justice for his chosen ones, who cry out to him day and night? Will he keep putting them off? I tell you, he will see that they get justice, and quickly. However, when the Son of Man comes, will he find faith on the earth?" Luke 18:1-8*

"Then Jesus said to them, 'Suppose you have a friend, and you go to him at midnight and say, 'Friend, lend me three loaves of bread; a friend of mine on a journey has come to me, and I have no food to offer him.' And suppose the one inside answers, 'Don't bother me. The door is already locked, and my children and I are in bed. I can't get up and give you anything.' I tell you, even though he will not get up and give you the bread because of friendship, yet because of your shameless audacity, he will surely get up and give you as much as you need. So I say to you: Ask and it will be given to you; seek and you will find; knock and the door will be opened to you. For everyone who asks receives; the one who seeks finds; and to the one who knocks, the door will be opened." Luke 11:5-10

"But as for you, be strong and do not give up, for your work will be rewarded." 2 Chronicles 15:7

"Let us not become weary in doing good, for at the proper time we will reap a harvest if we do not give up." Galatians 6:9

The Apostle Paul reminds us to "not lose heart" in the following two passages:

*"Therefore, since we have this ministry, as we received mercy, we **do not lose heart**, but we have renounced the things hidden because of shame, not walking in craftiness or adulterating the word of God, but by the manifestation of truth commending ourselves to every man's conscience in the sight of God." 2 Corinthians 4:1,2*

*"Therefore, we **do not lose heart**, but though our outer man is decaying, yet our inner man is being renewed day by day." 2 Corinthians 4:16*

So do not lose heart, choose to not give up, but let God renew you.

Make a Choice to Not Give Up

Will you choose to add perseverance to your life? A truly revived life, one that stays alive; only stays that way through perseverance. Maybe you have floundered for years, maybe you have been wishy-washy in your faith toward God. It's time to let bygones be bye and gone. It's time to become undead spiritually. God wants a thriving relationship with you, not a so-so one that you end up regretting in the end, one that you didn't put the effort into as you should have.

Are you going to let Satan lie to you or are you going to believe God? You need to make that choice. You need to pay back that little worm by not giving in, but by giving it all to God. Don't give up! Don't give up on your dreams, those things God has called you to. Don't give up hope! Satan will be defeated; God will rescue you and bring you through. God has great plans for your life. It's time to get fired up. Let the divine hand of God reach in with a poker and move the coals around so you can see the embers glow again. Don't give up!

3

FANNING THE FLAME

You are not going to be revived or be alive in your faith by sitting on the couch watching TV. Now that's a crazy statement to start this chapter with, but that is what the Lord just gave me tonight as I started this chapter. I thought it was important and it is. You see, I had a choice tonight. I could have vegged out after working all day, I could have watched the Tonight Show, or went on Facebook or played a video game, etc. But I knew I needed to get this done. I had a choice, and thankfully I decided to get going on this chapter instead of being distracted. I could have rested and wasted time that would have gained me nothing, or I could do God's will and do what He was speaking to my heart. I am glad that tonight I did His will, or He would have not given me this message about getting off the couch.

I should know about laying on the couch and watching TV or watching every movie that comes out, because I have done it for years. It has brought me no spiritual growth, nor has it helped me to fulfill the calling God has for my life. There is nothing wrong with rest and some down time in front of the TV, but too many of us American Christians (including myself) have fallen into the habit of doing it every night, or at least so often that our lives are passing us by, and I don't think this pleases God— that we waste our life watching silly productions, when we could be producing wealth in God's kingdom. I was convicted when I went to Mexico on our 20th anniversary. My wife and I met a local there who worked a full-time job after working at his family's farm all day. He said most Mexicans do not watch TV and sit on the couch. They usually work two or three jobs and would not even think about sitting around. Only one person in their town did, a wealthy person who never came out of his house. All he did was watch TV. We did observe this everywhere we went, they would be working one job, and then rush off to the next. I really learned something from the people of Mexico on that trip, but it has taken me a long time to even start to break the habit. First, I had to get the desire. Now I seem to be able to start breaking that habit more often. For some, you might say it is a sin to be repented from, not just a bad habit. So, I conclude with point one, here you can read it again "**You are not going to be revived or be alive in your faith by sitting on the couch watching TV**. It's in bold letters. Maybe God will speak to you like He has me. It's hard to hear when you are watching commercials.

Obtaining the Passionate Fire

I will never forget an experience I had while at Bible School with a fellow student, Russ Taylor. We had decided to pray for each other in the prayer room that was located on the first floor of our ten-story dorm. The first room was larger, with a smaller, connected room in the back. There had been a theme standing out through our speakers at school of the Fire of God, so we were praying for God's fire in our lives, His presence and work in us, that we would be fired up, that we would be full of His presence, that God would burn his passion in us. We went on for a while in intense prayer for ourselves and our student body. We seemed to sense His presence, and the room seemed to be getting hotter. As we concluded, another student who had been in the back room, came out sweating and passed by us to the door and complained, "Man, it's hot in here." We both broke out in laughter. It seemed God had answered our prayer by sending His Fire.

Desire the Fire. You can do your own study on the fire of God, and you will find it very enlightening. You can read in the Word of God in Deut. 4:24, 9:3 and Heb 10:31 that God is described as a "consuming fire" or like a "devouring fire" he would go ahead of the Children of Israel and burn everything that stood in their way. He consumes and destroys completely, everything that is not of Him. His Fire was His presence working to destroy falseness, and it can have that affect in our lives. We know that fire refines metals; it burns out the impurities...the dross. So does God's fire burn the impurities from our faith and from our hearts, so that all that is left is Him. Proverbs 17:3 says this: "*The crucible for silver and the furnace for gold, but the LORD tests the heart.*" We would do well if we often invite God's fire to test our hearts. We will experience His fire one way or another, I suggest we let His fire work now in our hearts.

Cultivating the Presence of God in Your Life

Through worship, God inhabits our praise. When we gather for prayer, He is in the midst, or when alone with Him when we hear that still small voice speaking to us.

He touches us. We are emotional beings created by God. We do not walk by our emotions, nor should we be led by them, but they are how we are wired to react, with emotion. That's how I am when I sense God's overwhelming presence: it brings tears to my eyes; it changes my heart. It usually encourages me to do God's will when I feel his presence. We don't live by feeling, but I do know when He is there, and it can affect us emotionally. One of the best emotions I have experienced in life is that closeness of His love so strong.

We don't seek the presence or the feeling. We seek Him, and he comes. If you have not experienced this, I would ask you to ask Him to meet you in person...with His presence. You can cultivate your heart so that He can touch you through worship, prayer and time listening to Him.

Have you ever seen someone passionate about something? You might say "they are on fire." There is a flame burning inside them that keeps them going strong, like the furnace of an old steam train, the hotter the coals get, the faster and stronger the engine runs. That fire, I believe, is our faith, it is something you cannot see, but it drives us to do things we have not done before. It is like that with God; He has given us a measure of faith. Romans 12:3. Here is where the "fanning the flame" comes into action. Paul tells Timothy in 2 Timothy 2:6 "*to **fan into flame** the gift of God, which is in you*" Paul then said it was through the laying on of hands that Timothy received the gift. The word "gift" in Greek is "Charisma." A gift is something given by grace from God, for use by the Holy Spirit in the churches. In verse five, Paul says "*I am reminded of your sincere faith.*" and for that reason, Paul reminds him to fan into flame this gift. The gifts of God are really gifts of grace given through faith. These gifts are nothing to boast about; nothing in us caused this gift. It is from God, but we can get more passionate about it. We can rekindle it. We can blow on it and get it going again. Some versions of the bible even say to rekindle or to stir up the gift of God within you. If you have ever tried to get a fire going again after it had died down, you know what to do, stir the coals a little and blow on them to get the flame going again. At our house, we have a fire pit in the backyard, and some young people were over for a fire. I had trimmed some bushes that day and had them in the pit, so they tried to get a fire going with these green branches on top. They put paper and sticks underneath, but the branches would not burn. After about a half hour, they were getting really frustrated that they couldn't get a fire going. Finally, one of the guys had a battery powered pump in his car that he used for camping to blow up things up with. He directed the air on the coals of paper and sticks they had tried to get going, and it was amazing what the blast of air did. Not only did it get the fire going, it was like a flame thrower. It made the flames shoot up so high that everyone had to move away. It was like a magical device that instantly got the flames to grow. Sometimes, we need to do this in our lives with the gift of faith God has given us. We need to get it going into a flame by stoking it and blowing some air on it. If the fire has really died down, this can take more effort, and sometimes, we just need to stir it a little and get a little air in there. The fact is, we need to fan it, to stir it, to get it going. God has given us free will and is not going to do everything for us. He expects us to stir ourselves up, to get the passion back and get on fire for Him.

Before You Get Stoned

Let me quote one of my favorite passages in the Bible that is found in 1 Samuel 30:6. The King James Version puts it so clearly:

*"And David was greatly distressed; for the people spake of stoning him, because the soul of all the people was grieved, every man for his sons and for his daughters: **but David encouraged himself in the LORD his God.**"*

David was in big trouble. Everyone was mad at him and about to stone him, but he encouraged himself in the Lord. When you are about to die, or you are just in trouble, you need to encourage yourself in the Lord. The first place we should go when in trouble is to God. You are going to face things in your life (if you haven't already) that will shake your faith or cause you to want to give up. This is when you really need to fan the flame. You may do it by hearing God's Word (*"So faith comes from hearing, and hearing through the word of Christ."* Rom. 10:17 ESV) or you may do it by prayer or spending time in His presence, or you may do it by praising Him, remembering Him, or taking a step of faith and believing Him. Whatever it takes to strengthen ourselves, to encourage ourselves in God, we need to do it. The power comes from Him, the increase comes from Him, the fire came from Him, but he doesn't force us. We have a choice. We can choose to keep our faith and gifts alive or let them die. David chose to be revived and strengthened himself in the Lord. We need to encourage ourselves in God.

Why Do We Need to Fan the Flame?

Here are four reasons we need to fan the flame:

1. **The fire can go out, if we don't fan it.** There is a danger of the gift dying out in us. We can become lazy and neglect it, and it will go out while we sleep. Paul told Timothy in 1 Timothy 4:14, **Don't neglect the fire.** The world will try to smother our fire out, or water it down, so that it goes out or becomes ineffective. It takes time and effort to keep the fire going. It can go out if we are not diligent in keeping it going.
2. **The Flame is to be shared.** God gives us life and gifts to share, not to hoard them or boast about them. If we don't use the gifts

to strengthen the body of Christ and build it up (Eph. 4:12) (I Cor. 14:21), then we aren't sharing it correctly or fairly, and our gifts and abilities will sit on a shelf collecting dust. Eventually, we will lose that gift in a sense by not using it. Our confidence will be lost, windows of opportunity will be lost, lives that could have been touched will be lost. We should look for ways to share the gifts God has given us. We need to fan the flame, so we can keep those gifts blazing for the maximum potential. There are people out there needing what we have. Don't let the devil tell you that you are not important.

3. **The Flame of God's presence enables you to do His work.** The Presence of God is given to do the work! It is not given so that you can sit there and ignore it. Don't ever take lightly God's presence, fire or desire He put's in you. Moses went up the mountain to meet with God. He experienced God's presence, then he came off the mountain and did the work God called him to do. The early church waited for the gift of the Holy Spirit. Once they were baptized in it, they went out and brought the gospel out to the world. We cannot do anything for God in our own strength; we have to be full of His Spirit and power. There is a time to pray and wait on God and then there is a time to go in the strength and fire He provides. The work of God is not always pretty or fun, but
when you are filled with God's Fire, it makes it possible and makes an impact beyond your own abilities. Doing God's work in your own strength is just work, but with the fire it is super-powered, and you are able to get it done. The end goal of fanning the flame is not for your own pleasure of experiencing God's presence, but so that you go out in His power and be equipped to do His will. His presence and fire should spur a going out, a sharing of the gift He's put in you. The fanning is done in the inner room; the result comes in the streets. There is a reason for the presence of God. It brings revival.

Inner Revival

4. **Being on Fire brings joy.** Nobody gets anything out of a fire that goes out and won't stay lit. They do, however, receive great joy from a fire that roars, a fire that puts out warmth and a nice flame. Besides others benefitting from a nice fire, you will benefit by knowing that you are being faithful with the gift God has given. Since God is the provider and enabler of the gifts, you will get great joy out of being a faithful steward of that gift. One of the greatest joys you can experience in this life is to have a fully fanned flame, operating in a fully functional gift of God, being a vessel that carries the message that saves lives.

One of the greatest experiences I had that brought the joy of God was in the early eighties on our way to share the gospel. A few of my friends would go on the weekend to Mooney Blvd. in Visalia, California to share the good news of Jesus with the young people. Mooney Blvd. was a very popular place to cruise cars and party in the parking lots, in fact people would come from L.A. two hundred and fifty miles away to cruise there. We had heard Arthur Blessit (the man who carried a cross around the world- see blessitt.com) who used a large wooden cross to draw people and be a witness for Christ. So, we made our own wooden cross out of some 4 X 4 wood that was laying in the backyard and put a skateboard truck on the bottom so it could roll because it was very heavy to drag all night. This particular night, we loaded the cross on top of a VW van and headed to Visalia from Hanford CA. I think there were about six of us, and we had prayed for the night and were singing praise songs in the van when it happened. We were intensely praising God and were fired up to see souls saved. As we were singing and worshipping, all of the sudden it felt as if God poured liquid joy down upon our van. We all started laughing so hard as we felt the pure joy of God. So much so that the driver had to pull over; he could not drive. It was I guess what some would call being drunk in the Spirit. God's presence was so strong that all we could do was sit there and laugh and thank Him for several minutes. We then took off again toward Visalia, and you should have seen the boldness and joy we had that night. We were yelling out the windows to people that Jesus loved them as we rolled onto the boulevard. We had a great night and got to pray for a lot of people that night. Many came to the cross that night for prayer and to talk. We knew that God had filled us with His joy so that we could boldly go into that dark area and be strong lights for His Glory.

Never Be Lacking in Zeal

There was a Christian song we used to sing in church. The first verse went like this...

> *The zeal of God has consumed me*
> *Deep within my soul*
> *A raging fire that keeps*
> *burning A fire that cannot be*
> *quenched*

Is it still true in the church, in your life? Have you lost zeal for God? Have you lost the burning fire deep inside your heart? Maybe it's time to rekindle it. Ask God to get it going again. If you never had it, maybe it's time to ask God to set a fire in you by His Holy Spirit. So often, we get so excited about trivial things like sports, or music, a movie or a new purchase, but we fail to get excited about what God has done, We don't even bother to find out more about Him. Paul said this in Romans 12:11: "**Never be lacking in zeal, but keep your spiritual fervor, serving the Lord.**" This verse really says it all when you break it down. In the Greek, "lacking" means lagging behind, sluggish or slothful or backward. I don't know about you, but I don't want to be the one lagging behind. I don't want to be going backwards either, so this verse tells us to not be lacking; Don't be lagging behind in zeal. Zeal here, is the word for diligence, meaning to make haste. So don't be lagging behind in your diligence, your earnestness in serving the Lord. We should be putting our love for the Lord first, and we should be diligent about it, in a hurry always to serve Him. Keep your Spiritual Fervor, it says. This word has the meaning of hot, as in boiling water. Keep it boiling, don't let your diligence cool down. If you really love someone, you won't let your love grow cold, you won't let it slip. So how do you do this? How do you keep this passion for the Lord? I am not going to give you five ways to keep your zeal for the Lord. It is something you need to keep up; it's something you need to do. Just do it, or you will be always lagging behind. Passion is something that comes and goes, and we don't always feel the passion, but we cannot let it slip from us and allow ourselves to go backwards. We have to do what it takes to keep that water boiling. If it has gone cold, then we need to get that fire going again. I cannot tell you how to do that, but I can tell you that you need to do it. Other chapters in this book may help you to get that fire going, but you have to choose to do it, to be diligent about it. It must come from deep within your soul. It must be that important, that you dig deep until it is hot. Don't take the kettle off the stove too often or early. Do what it takes to get it to boil. If you need help, then I would ask God for help. That's what I do, and he always restores my zeal if I have let it cool off. But the point is to keep it, don't let yourself slip. If you have, then get that urgency back and keep it. He loves us so much. There is no amount of effort that compares with what he has done for us, but it will take effort on your part to make sure your zeal for God does not wane, but is always fervently hot!

David sang in Psalm 69: "*for zeal for your house consumes me*" and the disciples remembered this verse when Jesus overturned the tables in the temple in John 2:13-17. Do you have this kind of jealousy for God's house that David sang about? Farther down in Psalm 69, David says this in verses 30-32:

> "*I will praise God's name in song and glorify him with thanksgiving. This will please the* Lord *more than an ox, more than a bull with its horns and hooves. The poor will see and be glad— you who seek God, may your hearts*
> *live!*"

Maybe it is time to start worshipping Him, to praise God's name in song and glorify him with thanksgiving. Maybe it's time to let your heart live again and be on fire for him. Maybe it's time to fan the flame.

Be a Punk

    Punks are sticks used for lighting fireworks. They are safer than a match or a lighter because they can be held at a longer distance to light things. They last longer, so you don't need to keep using matches. A punk that you get to light fireworks remains glowing after being lit. It is always ready to light things. Its heat lasts for a long time. A firework makes a big flash or sound, then it is gone, but the punk stays lit for the entire show. Its constant burning comes from the intense flame it took to light it before the show. The punk is able to light big fireworks, even though it is just a cheap stick covered in manure or sawdust. Once it is lit, you blow on it, and it just gets hotter. The punk has the potential to set the world on fire. Be like a firework punk. Let God light you, and keep you going so that you are always ready to light up your world.

    Be Passionate for God. He is passionate about you. and don't forget to fan the flame and let God light up your life again!

4

TIME ALONE

This is where you hear from God. Where you wrestle with Him, and He works the things out of your heart that are wrong and puts in you the things that are on His heart. This place can be the most memorable of all. It can be the most motivating of all. Time alone with God is definitely the most life changing. Just you and God, spending time together. Spending time alone with God is probably the most important practice that will bring you into a personal revival, and as a result will allow the Spirit of God to overflow in your life so that you can be used in a public revival.

The message in Chapter 10 that you will read later only came about by time spent alone with God, time that was set aside to hear from Him. If you don't set aside time to spend with God, it is very hard to know His will and what He wants done. If you don't listen to God when you are alone, you won't be able to listen when you are with others, and you won't be able to do what He wants. God longs for us to come to Him and spend time with Him. Jesus modeled this. He would have done nothing without spending time with God, and he did nothing without learning it from his Father. So, Jesus said, *"When you have lifted up the Son of Man, then you will know that I am He and that I do nothing on my own but speak just what the Father has taught me." John 8:28*

Jesus, the Model

Following are some verses from the Bible on how Jesus spent time alone with the Father.

"After he had dismissed them, he went up on a mountainside by himself to pray. Later that night, he was there alone." Matthew 14:23

"Very early in the morning, while it was still dark, Jesus got up, left the house and went off to a solitary place, where he prayed." Mark 1:35

"Immediately Jesus made his disciples get into the boat and go on ahead of him to Bethsaida, while he dismissed the crowd. After leaving them, he went up on a mountainside to pray." Mark 6:45-46

"At daybreak, Jesus went out to a solitary place. The people were looking for him and when they came to where he was, they tried to keep him from leaving them." Luke 4:42

"But Jesus often withdrew to lonely places and prayed." Luke 5:16

"One of those days Jesus went out to a mountainside to pray, and spent the night praying to God." Luke 6:12

I encourage you to take time, to make time, to be alone with God.

The Hardest Thing

When you set yourself to spend time alone with God, you will find it is the hardest thing to do. You will find out how hard of a pull the world has on you. Distractions of all kinds seem to come into our lives. Spending time with God not only shows us how strong the world's grasp is on us is, but the time spent with God will help us break the hold the world has on us. I have to admit; this has probably been the hardest struggle in my life to overcome: consistently spending time alone with God. After 30 years of following Jesus, I have finally incorporated a mostly consistent daily prayer time with God, but to spend long periods of time with God is still an area I struggle with. I feel I should be doing something, accomplishing something, not just spending time alone; but what could be more important than time with God? I am preaching to myself now, and in the writing of this chapter, I can see my need for this practice. Like I said before, this is probably the hardest practice to accomplish, but most assuredly the most beneficial and rewarding. Every time I do put everything else aside and seek God, I always walk away more encouraged, more passionate and more motivated to do what I should be doing. We cannot expect to have any kind of revival if we are not willing to spend our time with the master of the universe, with our loving heavenly Father, who wants us to spend time with Him.

Get Away from the World

Sometimes you need to get away from the world. The influence of the world can lull you into a routine to where you just conform to the pattern of the world. Too many people get into a busy routine- work, doing what everyone else is doing, watching tv, but it takes a daring soul, a live soul, to go to the lonely place, where God is heard. So, you need to get outside the box of the world system. You need to get to a quiet place because if you don't, the noise will cause you to settle for the sounds around you, instead of seeking to hear the still small voice of the Lord. (read 1 Kings 19:11-13) It takes discipline to get away from the world and to hear from God. It takes action and response to get alone. It's not an easy thing, but if you want to stay alive, you had better do it. The world and people will change you if you don't get away and let God change you. Don't fool yourself, friendship with the world will drag you down, Time alone with God will renew you!

> *"Do not love the world or anything in the world. If anyone loves the world, love for the Father is not in them." 1 John 2:15*

The Burning Bus

The benefits of spending time with God are life changing and unforgettable. When I was a young man, I attended an outreach in Hollywood with Y.W.A.M (Youth With a Mission). I saw God do amazing things as we set out to be witnesses for Jesus in some of the darkest places of Los Angeles. We shared the love of Christ with prostitutes, runaways and street people. For some dumb reason on the way back to our base one night, I was doubting what God's plan was for me. While riding the big school bus back, I was wanting to know if the Great Commission (Matthew 28:19,20) Jesus gave was really for us Christians today, and for me personally…not just for the disciples that were with Jesus. I was really seeking God for an answer. Even amidst the chatter and excitement on the bus, I was able to spend time alone with God and really seek Him. I opened my Bible and was led to read the story Jesus told about the good Samaritan in Luke 10:25-37. I will never forget the last words of that story that jumped off the page: *"Go and do likewise."* God had answered my question personally to me. There on that crowded bus as his child, I asked him a burning question, and He burned the answer into my heart and mind. You can make time to be alone with God even if it is on a bus.

A little later in my life, I knew I had to spend time with God as a busy Dad. We lived in a small town, but life was busy and at that stage in life, I knew I needed to get alone with God. As one pastor of mine, Bill Black, had said "You need to come apart, or you will come apart." Life's business and stresses can tear us apart if we do not spend time with our Father, who gives us the wisdom and strength that we need to make it in this world.

On several occasions, I would ride my mountain bike up a big hill to the golf course late at night to spend some time in prayer after a busy day. As I would come over this big hill in the darkness, there was a small pond with a large water fountain in it. The fountain was lit up with red lights in it. I would stop on the side of the hill, looking down at the glowing red fountain. It reminded me of the burning bush that Moses saw. It was a little spooky with the dark trees around the golf course, but it was a great place to get alone with God and pray. Many times, God would touch my heart there and give me answers to prayer or would encourage me to keep pressing on. I will never forget the burning bush (fountain). So, if it is on a bus, near a fountain, in the wilderness, or in your bedroom, you need to take time out of your busy schedule to really come away and be with God alone, face-to-face, heart-to-heart. Then you will know the truth, then you will know God. Don't expect to know him if you aren't willing to take the time to do so.

Recently, I experienced a loss of my job of almost 15 years. I thought it would be no problem landing a job in a thriving job market. To my surprise, it was not. This caused me to pray a little harder, to spend a little more time with God, which I should have been doing all along. It is easy to fall into discouragement and depression when you are going through a loss of any kind. So far, my experience has shown me that I have to really seek God in these times. When I am down, I need to go to the one who will lift me up. I found this great lesson out, and it is this: When you are down and nobody seems to be on your side, when you feel all alone, and things are not working out for you, this is the time to get alone with God. **When you are truly alone, this is when He, alone, shows you His Power and encouragement and guidance.** You have to get alone with Him, and you have to stay there until you hear from Him. And even if you don't hear a thing, His presence and power will change you and make you stronger. You have to go there; you have to Seek Him.

Seeking God

The whole point here is what the Bible talks about a lot; seeking God. You have to actively seek him if you want to find Him. If you are on crowded bus or at a park at night, it takes an active, purposed, effort on your part to seek God. Don't expect to be revived without that. So many people I meet have so many questions about life, but they never take a moment and really seek God for the answer. Our flesh wants to do things the fleshly way. We don't want to take the time to really give ourselves to God. I hope that you will not make that mistake. Start now, and don't stop seeking God; quit trying to do everything your way, and seek Him until He shows you how to do it His way. He will answer you. Take a look at these verses on Seeking God.

"Look to the LORD and his strength; seek his face always." 1 Chronicles 16:10

"And you, my son Solomon, acknowledge the God of your father, and serve Him with wholehearted devotion and with a willing mind, for the LORD searches every heart and understands every motive behind the thoughts. If you seek Him, He will be found by you; but if you forsake Him, He will reject you forever." I Chronicles 28:9

"If my people, who are called by my name, will humble themselves and pray and seek my face and turn from their wicked ways, then will I hear from heaven and will forgive their sin and will heal their land." II Chronicles 7:14

"Those who know your name will trust in you, for you, LORD, have never forsaken those who seek you." Psalm 9:10

"The LORD looks down from heaven on the sons of men to see if there are any who understand, any who seek God." Psalm 14:2

"The lions may grow weak and hungry, but those who seek the LORD lack no good thing." Psalm 34:10

"Blessed are they who keep His statutes and seek Him with all their heart." Psalm 119:2

"I love those who love me, and those who seek me find me." Proverbs 8:17

"Seek the LORD while He may be found; call on Him while He is near." Isaiah 55:6

"You will seek me and find me when you seek me with all your heart."
Jeremiah 29:13

"Ask and it will be given to you; seek and you will find; knock and the door will be opened to you. For everyone who asks receives; the one who seeks finds; and to the one who knocks, the door will be opened." Matthew 7:7

"So I say to you: Ask and it will be given to you; seek and you will find; knock and the door will be opened to you. For everyone who asks receives; the one who seeks finds; and to the one who knocks, the door will be opened." Luke 11:9-10

*"God did this so that men would **seek** Him and perhaps reach out for Him and find Him, though He is not far from each one of us." Acts 17:27*

"And without faith it is impossible to please God, because anyone who comes to Him must believe that He exists and that He rewards those who earnestly seek Him." Hebrews 11:6

These are just a few verses that encourage us to seek the Lord. You might want to do a study in the Bible on the word seek to find more or look up the word seek in a Bible concordance and read through the verses from time to time.

Before we go onto the next Chapter and try to accomplish something great, we must first commit to this one thing and do it. Again, if we heed the words of Pastor Bill, " Come apart, or you will come apart." So, come apart from everything and spend time alone with God, and we can be sure that this is one of the fastest and most guaranteed ways to get revived if you are dead spiritually. So, stop right now! Block out all the temporal things and spend some time alone with God; you will not regret it. Make this a habit in your life; instead of turning elsewhere, turn to God alone.

5

GO TIME

God's heart is to reach every person with the Good News. Our job is to go. There are many reasons that stop us from doing this.

We know it was the final commission of Jesus to send us into the entire world with the Gospel—the Good News. Our responsibility is to speak for Him, to reach the lost. We are his body. How much learning is enough? How much fellowship; how much studying; how much do we need to be babied, before we get going? The calling of the church is not to stay; it is not to sit still. It is to go. We know there is work to do, but we just can't get ourselves to do it. We want to make sure, to get everything right, so much so that we never venture out of our little rooms or our big auditoriums.

This is a missing part of many churches today. There is something more than just going to church on Sunday. That something is reaching out with the Gospel. We tend to want to draw the unsaved into our world, get them working for our little group, but we never purposefully go out into the world to rescue those who are dying. If we merely focus on ourselves to become better Christians but never venture out of our church building, what good are our beliefs? What would happen? What if we did share the Gospel? What if we were the Good Samaritans?

Have you ever shared the Gospel to the lost and experienced being used of God to minister to someone? Have you ever reached out of your own world and brought the love of God to someone else? Have you ever become "others aware" instead of just being "self-aware?" When you focus on the needs of others, suddenly you realize the big picture, and you are used by God to fulfill His purpose, not yours. If you have done this, you know it is probably the most fulfilling thing that can happen to you. The most humbling, and yet the most satisfying to your spirit; nothing else matters. It takes a going to experience this. It just doesn't happen by sitting there observing and learning. It takes a going.

Get Rid of the Limiter

What stops you from going? What really keeps you from being revived and doing God's will.

Ephesians 6:12 tells us that our struggle is not against flesh and blood:

> *"For our struggle is not against flesh and blood, but against the rulers, against the authorities, against the powers of this dark world, and against the spiritual forces of evil in the heavenly realms."*

As we talked about Satan's schemes in Chapter 2, and from this verse, we see that he is behind what causes us to struggle. He uses sin to bring us down and defeat us. We do have a choice though; God has given us free will and the ability to make choices. We don't have to sin. Jesus has paid the price for sin and gives us the power through His blood to overcome it.

To say that sin limits us is an understatement. Sin separates us from God. (Isaiah 59:2) So if we are separated from God, how can we be revived, and how can we fulfill His purpose and will on the earth? We need to get rid of the limiter.

Since we are still living in this body that is susceptible to sin and temptation, we are susceptible to being limited. I am still tempted to this day with the sin of stealing. Yes, after following Christ for years, my flesh is still tempted with what I can get away with. You see, when I was younger, I fell to the sin of stealing, and it kept growing, even though I knew it was wrong. Once I started following Christ, I stopped stealing, but the temptation still hits me. When I see an armored car, I start to imagine how I could get away with a heist. It appeals to my flesh to do something like that and get away with it. Recently, I had this thought, and the Lord reminded me that not stealing is one of His main commandments. *"Thou shalt not steal."* I repented again for even having the thought and could see how my flesh has had this tendency to sin all these years. It limited me because I thought it was me wanting to commit a crime, but I realized it was temptation appealing to my sinful nature, not who I am in Christ.

Maybe you are not tempted with stealing, maybe it's gossiping, and you are tempted all the time to talk bad about your co-workers or people in your community. When we are in sin, and we are not being revived on a daily basis, we tend to be depressed, or we find fault with others to take the blame off ourselves. Maybe it is smoking that keeps you in bondage, or alcohol, or lust, or lying. Sin can also be not doing what we ought to. Oops, you didn't want to hear that, did you? (*"If anyone, then, knows the good they ought to do and doesn't do it, it is sin for them." James 4:17*) Some sins can take a lifetime to break off us, some take a second. The temptation may be there your whole life on this earth, but you have to stop it, (even if it takes 70 years, it will be worth it) because it is limiting you. Sin is a terrible Task Master; it makes you do things you really didn't want to. When sin rules, we lose. We cannot be used of God fully when we are tangled up by sin. His word tells us not to let this happen.

We are all tempted, and we all sin, but Christ cleanses us from that sin. (1 John 1:8, 9)

We can get out; we can overcome through the power of Christ. It's not our righteousness but His that gets us out. But He expects us to choose not to allow it to rule us and not to live in it.

The famous verse from the book of Hebrews 12:1 tells us to *"throw off everything that hinders and the sin that so easily entangles."* And here is another interesting verse: *"Therefore do not let sin reign in your mortal body so that you obey its evil desires." Romans 6:12*

Do something to get rid of sin in your life and keep it away. This is a sure-fire way to lead to revival. Put yourself in a position to win. Like a runner in a sprint gets out the blocks and positions them to race. Put yourself in the position to go; be ready always; don't let sin bog you down or chain your foot from running the race any more.

I like what Peter says at the end of 2 Peter 3:14 *"Make every effort to be found spotless, blameless and at peace with him."*

The best way to start if you are struggling with temptation and sin, is to make every effort, but only Jesus can help us. We must go to him for help. Only he can help us; we cannot do it on our own. Our race to conquer sin must start with him. Ask Him to help you and keep asking Him until he gives you the strength. Those principalities and powers are very strong, but God is stronger. Make every effort, and don't give up. Only He can make you spotless and blameless. There is more in the Bible on conquering sin and how to do that, but here, the point is simple, it needs to go.

One of my favorite encounters Jesus had was with the woman in John chapter 8. She was caught in adultery and brought to Jesus to see if He would approve of her being stoned to death as the law of Moses said. Jesus said to those who accused her *"Let any one of you who is without sin be the first to throw a stone at her."* I will let you read the rest in verses 9-11:

> *"At this, those who heard began to go away one at a time, the older ones first, until only Jesus was left, with the woman still standing there. Jesus straightened up and asked her, 'Woman, where are they? Has no one condemned you?'*
>
> *'No one, sir,' she said.*
>
> *'Then neither do I condemn you,' Jesus declared."*

I don't think I have ever been able to read this account without shedding a tear because of how forgiving God is toward us, but then he finishes in verse 11 with these encouraging words to the woman... **"Go now and leave your life of sin."** I don't believe He would have said that to her if it were not possible. She could go now, and leave that life of sin. Jesus forgave her and had given her what she needed to live a new life. So, go now and leave sin behind you.

More Than Seeing the Need

It takes seeing the need to get you going. To get motivated to go, you need to see the need. But to really go and to keep going, you have to have this thing called a burden for the lost. Jesus knew we were all lost at some point. Someone needs to find us. We are called to be His ambassadors in 2 Corinthians 5:20 "*We are therefore Christ's ambassadors, as though God were making his appeal through us. We implore you on Christ's behalf: Be reconciled to God.*" It is our job to find the lost and share the Good News with them. We have to have that same burden that he had, that heart of love for the lost. But that is not all; if we see the need, we have to act, or we are worthless to the cause, and we have not obeyed God nor done his will. We are not obeying the greatest commandment found in Matthew 22:37 and 38 if we don't act on it. It is a command and our purpose to love God and love others as our self.

We can see all the need all we want, but if we don't go, what good are we? What have we done? It's like seeing someone that is about to get hit by a car, and we just sit on the curb watching. There comes a time that you can't watch anymore, you can't watch anyone else go to hell or be enslaved by the devil. You have to act; you have to go. You can spend your whole life studying the game, but to really be in the game you have to get off the bench. You have to physically get out there. You will learn as you go.

Like in worship, if you don't physically do something, you won't experience anything. If you don't physically go, you will never see what God wants to do. You go, he will provide. It never works the opposite way. You move; he works in you, through you and around you. Don't miss out on what God has, just go.

The first time I heard the phrase " It's go time." was when my boys and I were playing hockey with my brother in law, Scott. He would say "It's go time." as he would check one of us and score. The phrase is a slang term from the 80's, and if you research it, it is hard to find the true origin. Some say it was used in a fight; if someone was confronting you, it would be "go time." I always thought it was used in the military, as they were embarking on a mission, like when they were ready to jump out of a plane to confront the enemy. As Christians, we are in a fight, a battle for souls, a fight against evil, dark forces that can only be pushed back by the light of Christ in us. If we sit there and do nothing, if we don't jump out of the plane, then we will lose, and so will many others. We have to go; we have to go on the offense; we have to be proactive; we have to take the jump of faith and do something. One definition of "Go time" said that it means "time to get serious about doing something." I think that's why it was the last command Jesus impressed on His followers before He left. He wanted us to know that it is "Go Time." We are not meant to be disciples of His just to learn, but also to go. It's time to get serious about the great commission He gave us.

The Great Commission: Matthew 28:18-20

"Then Jesus came to them and said, 'All authority in heaven and on earth has been given to me. Therefore, go and make disciples of all nations, baptizing them in the name of the Father and of the Son and of the Holy Spirit, and teaching them to obey everything I have commanded you. And surely I am with you always, to the very end of the age.'"

Jesus did not say, go if it is convenient or if people are receptive. In our ever-changing world in which we live, it seems more difficult to obey the great commission. Many people today do not want to hear about Jesus; they do not want you knocking on their doors. They wouldn't answer anyway because they are either on their computers or tv's. And are too busy to listen. No, evangelism is not simple, but it is required; it is what we are supposed to be doing until Jesus returns. He has empowered us and equipped us with the Holy Spirit, so we are without excuse. The only thing we need to be is obedient. It is His plan; He came and died for the sins of the world; he left us with the task of sharing that Good News, and He will return. So, if you haven't started yet, it's time to get going.

Second Peter 3:8-9 says this:

"But do not forget this one thing, dear friends: With the Lord a day is like a thousand years, and a thousand years are like a day. The Lord is not slow in keeping His promise, as some understand slowness. Instead He is patient with you, not wanting anyone to perish, but everyone to come to repentance."

He hasn't come back yet because He is patiently waiting for everyone to come to repentance. But we know not everyone will obey and turn to Him. Not everyone will choose eternal life. But we must tell them how to find it. We must ask God for wisdom and for the courage to tell them. Their souls depend on it. They will not know, if we are not obedient and give them the message of His love and forgiveness. We have to show them the way, whatever it takes.

It's time to put the pedal to the metal and see what you've got. It's time to have faith. It's time to go! **IT'S GO TIME.**

Share the good news of Jesus Christ with the lost!

6

BLOOM AND BOOM WHERE YOU ARE PLANTED

Many chapters in books have been titled "Bloom Where You Are Planted" and I didn't want to use this title because I didn't want to copy others. I wasn't trying to copy anyone,
but I felt that this was a viable principle and topic that has some very important concepts to practice and live by and that we should be aware of, if we want to be revived. It's kind of like a process of doing it the right way and not jumping out because it's hard; just bloom where you are and grow now.

Bloom Where You're Planted and Use What You've Got.

This is a simple principle that simply means to grow and start where you are, and do it now. Don't keep thinking "if only this would happen" or "if I was in that situation I could grow." You need to soak in the light; you need to soak in the water and drink! Now is the time to bloom; don't wait until it's too late. What do you have to lose by waiting? You need to grow now, where you are, in spite of the circumstances you are in. You need to obey God now and start following Him. You can be alive; you can thrive; you can be revived!

I have heard it said that if a tree keeps getting transplanted, it won't grow. You need to grow in the situation God has you in, even if you are in a bad situation. God will bring you out, but you must not wait for everything to be perfect. Some of our best growth happens when we face hard times. When faced with tough situations, you can either learn and grow through it, or give up and die. The Bible tells us to choose life! Read Deuteronomy Chapter 30.

Recently I was growing tomato plants indoors so they could get an early start before I planted them outside. They tell you to have a fan on the plants when growing them indoors. I didn't understand why you would need a fan. I thought it was to blow the heat around or something like that, but actually, the reason is that it makes the plants stronger. When they are faced with wind, they strengthen themselves, so they can resist. When they are put outside, they don't wilt from the strong winds. Trials in life make us stronger; don't let them make you wilt and give up. You are meant to grow and bloom and bear fruit.

Check your attitude; is it right? The circumstances you are in don't seem to be fair, so are you making the best out of it? Are you being your best, or have you fallen to your circumstances? Are you making the right choices? Are you choosing life?

Be a Good Steward of What You've Been Given.

It is a great honor to be breathing. You know that you did not have to be born. There is a reason you have been given this one life, and it's not to waste it. You have been given something more valuable than any wealth, and that is life itself. It's an opportunity God has given each of us, and it is what we do with it that matters. You have one life, and you can either sit there and do nothing with it, or you can take risks and invest it.

In Matthew 25:14-30, Jesus gives the famous parable about the talents. Talents were money, but we can apply this to our life as well. In the first verse of the parable, Jesus tells of a man who was going on a journey and entrusted his possessions to his three servants. When he returned, he found that two of them had invested what he had given them to gain more. The one who only had one talent buried it instead of investing it. The man was furious with the lazy one and had him thrown out. You must use the life and talents God has given you now. Invest yourself. Don't wait for everything to go your way. Trust God now and use what you have been given.

Use What You've Got

In 1 Samuel 17:37-40, David went to battle with what God had given him, instead of someone else's armor. King Saul dressed David in his own clothes and armor to defeat Goliath, but David was not used to the armor and could not walk around in it. So, he took off Saul's armor and used what he had: a sling and stones. People are always wanting you to do things with what they have, or do things the way they would do it. They want to put in there two cents, even though they are not the ones stepping out with their lives. You need to be careful taking things from others that you are not used to, doing things the way they demand you do it. They want a stake in it, but aren't willing to take the risk. I have noticed whenever I want to take a risk that may have a great outcome, that there are always people who will try to keep me from doing it. They will try to tell you how to do it, or they will try to stop you from doing it. It is almost a joke because they aren't willing to do anything, but they want to give their advice. Never take that advice. Only take Godly advice and weigh it to see if it lines up with God's word, will and purpose. If it only lines up with fear and doubt or confusion, pay it no mind, and do what the Holy Spirit is prompting you to do. So, David went with what he had: his staff and his sling, and he put the stones in his shepherd bag. You know the rest of the story. He defeated Goliath. You have gifts and talents that you are used to. Look around and see what you have and start with what you know and then trust God to use you.

Bloom and Boom

A fireworks display does not happen by chance. The fireworks have to be made correctly with the right powder. They have to be set up so the timing is perfect. This comes by preparing in the right way. Mistakes can be costly and dangerous. So those who want to finish well, will take care in the steps of preparation. A person should use the correct resources they have in a correct way. This applies to our life and faith. We have been given a life and a measure of faith, but we can use it haphazardly and carelessly. We can fall into the trap of thinking we don't have to do it right, or we can cut corners. Just as with fireworks, this could result in a disaster and could affect a lot of people around you. But using what you have in the correct way, with utmost care and dedication, can change the lives of others who are looking to see what is possible in life.

Prepare Now

"God doesn't bless an empty mind.", one of my college teachers said. God gave you a brain for a reason. Don't be careless with it, and don't play around. God does not usually bless someone and give them a thriving, abundant life, if they don't use what he gave them correctly. I heard a college professor say this once, and he was correct. If you want to be successful, then you must prepare. You don't go up against Goliath until you have gone down to the river and selected your stones. You can't give a good sermon, write a good book, give a good speech, or reach people in any form, if you do not prepare well. In fact, I believe to the extent you prepare will be the extent you make an impact. Say, for instance, you want to help the homeless. If you don't research to find out their needs and what could help them, you won't be of much help to them.

Be obedient with what God puts before you. Prepare, grow and do it right!

Push Back the Dirt

Think of a seed planted in the ground. The seed is dormant for a long time. As it is warmed and watered, it begins to grow roots and starts growing. A stem starts to grow upward. That seed needs to push through the dirt. It eventually makes it through to the sunlight, where it develops leaves and branches and eventually bears fruit. We can be like that seed. We can lay there in the dirt, or we can decide to grow, to push upward. There is a lot of dirt on some of us. We need to push through the dirt, through the negative, through the weights, through the dark, until we get to the sunlight. It's do or die. Faith is like a seed; it has to grow. It just can't stay in the ground. Some of you have been trampled on, pushed down, buried too deep, given no water, and just want to sit in the darkness and only dream of bearing fruit someday. It is time for you to lift your little head up, to start stretching as hard as you can for the surface. It's time to rise; it's time to break through the dirt. It's time to use the God-given strength and faith you have been given and live. Don't stay in the dirt one more second. Don't let the life in you die in the ground. It's time to grow into the beautiful plant you were meant to be. Open up your hands to God and Glorify Him with your life. Spread your arms out like branches, and touch the world. Reach out to God, and give Him the Glory!

Make Revival a Habit in Your Life

Train for Godliness. Don't let people get you off your spiritual walk with God. Don't let people keep you from God, and don't let people keep you from being revived by God. There will always be critics of those who follow God. Do not waste your time trying to do things their way, when you know what God wants you to do. Don't get off track with God; make sure you are doing what it takes now to be close to God, that you are making your abundant life in Christ a habit, in fact your main habit, in life. Of all the habits to have, a habit of revival is one that will never let you down.

Anyone can be dead; not everyone is in the habit of being alive. So, train yourself to be Godly, just as people hit the gym to stay in shape. Don't let yourself get out of shape with God because of people or circumstances; stay in God's gym. He's the best trainer. And if you have been away from him, now is the time to get your soul back to the gym. Your personal trainer is waiting for you.

Boom Where You Are Planted

So, wherever you are is where God has you, even though it might not be where you want to be. Be obedient, and be the best example you can for Christ. Be the best role model, the best example to others. Don't cave and become like the world and those who live in darkness. If you have read the story of Joseph in the Bible, you know he was put into very bad situations in his life. He was sold into slavery by his brothers, was set up by his bosses' wife, was put in prison, but he chose to make his life boom where he was. He impacted those around him instead of letting those people and his circumstances stop him from doing God's will and fulfilling God's purpose for him. Read his story starting in Genesis 37 and ending in Genesis 50:20, where he said these famous words to his brothers, "*You intended to harm me, but God intended it for good to accomplish what is now being done, the saving of many lives.*"

When the normal gets boring, and there's nothing left; when everyone is against you, learn to rely on and trust God so that when He does call you to move on into tougher areas, or into the promised land, you have already come to trust him in the mundane. Know that only he can do things; only he can cause growth, save people and through experience in the wilderness, He has proven that he always will be there. He will never leave or forsake you. When you know that there's no one else to go to, no one else you can rely on, then you will really grow and be used of Him. Then you will really boom and make an impact on those around you.
"*Physical training is good, but training for godliness is much better, promising benefits in this life and in the life to come.*" 1 Timothy 4:8 NLT

7

THE POWER IS ESSENTIAL – THE POWER OF THE HOLY SPIRIT

Many people know about Jesus Christ and believe in Him. They even live for Him and are active in ministry. But to stay active, vibrant, consistent, on fire, stoked, revived, you need the Holy Spirit; you need the Baptism of the Holy Spirit.

Katherine Kuhlman called the Holy Spirit the key to her ministry, the giver of the gifts. That statement intrigued me, and I believed her. As I set out to write this chapter, I was not settled on what the content would be, but knew this was a true principle, and most likely the most important one discussed in this book.

I was thinking of the power of the Holy Spirit, the attributes of the Holy Spirit, how to be filled with the Holy Spirit. I thought of going through the book of Acts and quoting all the scriptures that have to do with the Holy Spirit and what the evidence of the Spirit was in the early Church. There are so many books on that subject, and if you are interested in being filled and baptized in the Holy Spirit, I suggest you get one of those and study it, but mainly just ask for the filling of the Holy Spirit if you want that. The only thing you really need to know is that you should ask for the Holy Spirit, and Jesus is the Baptizer. Luke 11:13, Luke 3:16, John 16:7, Luke 24:49. So, I will not go into great detail about it in this book, but will just try to explain the Holy Spirit's importance in having a vibrant, revived life.

So, in my seeking and pondering on what to write about the Holy Spirit, I have put off this chapter for probably a year. I have most of the content for the other chapters done, but had not started this one, nor did I know what to write. I wanted to experience and live these chapters and learn as I wrote, because we all know the teacher learns more than the students. If you have ever taught before, you know this is true. I knew the Lord wanted to teach me something about the Holy Spirit, and He would, but I felt I had really become undisciplined on the writing of this book. The desire was still there, but I have been putting it off, because I did not want to just write another book on the Holy Spirit. I wanted you, the reader, to know how important the Holy Spirit is. I could write volumes on the Holy Spirit and never do Him justice, and I did not want to do that. The Spirit seems to be like the wind; it blows where and when it wants. Most importantly, it blows when we need it.

I am very ecstatic now to write and very inspired now that I have started back, but it didn't come from self-motivation. It came from the Spirit's prompting and teaching. I am still unsure about everything I will write on this subject and that is the good thing about it. I am trying my hardest to follow the Spirit's leading in this so that you can be blessed by what you read.

Some of these things are a revelation to me at this present time. After researching the Bible, asking the Holy Spirit and praying, not specifically for this book, but part of my daily prayer, that I would be led by the Spirit and filled with the Spirit and Love of God.

First, I was praying more to be led by the Spirit, and it seemed that not much was happening for a while. However, recently I have been praying to be filled with the Holy Spirit, and it seems to me this has been answered. As I write this, I feel a strong anointing or influence of the Holy Spirit. It is almost like being intoxicated, so I am trying to write this while under this influence that is very strong at the moment. I don't know how it happened, but I have been desiring the presence of the Holy Spirit and to feel His Presence. Tonight, it did, and I believe the Holy Spirit brought things to my memory in a very empowering way.

It is exactly what I wanted to happen as I wrote this book. I wanted to experience revival; I wanted to live it, to write from experience. I wanted to know that this book was something true and not just ideas that popped into my head. I really want to live a revived, alive, life of faith that does God's will. I believe somehow, he used some messages I was watching of the late Kathryn Kuhlman. It was as though He was really speaking to me through her preaching. Some of the following writings in this section are things that jumped out to me about the Holy Spirit while listening to her messages. Then, I will conclude this chapter with some points that I believe were prompted by the Holy Spirit. I am not going to exhaust this topic, instead, I will just write what I feel the Spirit wants me to. If I were doing a scholarly study on the Holy Spirit, it would be a work in itself and be several volumes.

It's a Choice

The biggest thing that I learned from Miss Kuhlman's message was that the Holy Spirit does not force you to be filled, to be revived, or lead you. We want to be led by the Spirit, and scripture admonishes us to be filled with the Spirit and walk after the Spirit and not the flesh. It is very simple, and I thought it was so mystical to be led by the Spirit and hard to narrow it down. In fact, it is so simple to be led. All you have to do is follow! So, there you have it, such profoundness. We want to be led, then we have to follow. It's a choice, not something forced on you. You have to want it enough to follow, which means you have to give up other things; you can't follow one path if you are following others or being distracted by other things. You should not choose to be mind-led, or will-led, emotions-led, others-led, world-led, Satan-led or self-led. You have to choose to follow the Spirit of God and want His fullness more than anything else. Not so that you are filled to show off or show people how spiritual you are, but so you can please God alone and do His will. The Holy Spirit will help you love God more and love others like God would. You can't do anything in this Christian life that amounts to anything in your own power. It has to be the power of the Holy Spirit.

Nothing else matters, you see. You can study all you want, but if it is not done through the Spirit's Power, it is nothing. You cannot revive yourself. The dead bones don't come alive by your spirit. Life can only be given by God's Spirit. So, all the other principles in this book mean nothing if you are not following the Holy Spirit. Keeping in step with the Spirit means following, not leading. In essence, all of the other principles in this book have nothing to do with self-effort, but a reliance on the Spirit. Yes, you have to make a choice to seek God, to step up, to go, but it's all got to be by the Holy Spirit's empowerment and direction. Being obedient to the Spirit's direction and guidance is why you should desire to be revived and filled. Otherwise, your searching is in vain. The gift of the Holy Spirit is what gives you life; it is what gives the body its power.

The Holy Spirit is what changed the disciples into world changers. Without the Holy Spirit, Christianity is just another form of religion. You need the Holy Spirit if you are going to follow God, and you need to follow the Holy Spirit if you want to follow God. Kathryn Kuhlman knew and said that "the key to the power is the Holy Spirit." Nothing else.

If you are going to try another way, you will be sadly disappointed. If you try to manufacture your life in any other way, it will fail. The Holy Spirit is the key to your life.

I have found this to be true in my life, that when the Holy Spirit is doing the leading and I am following, I obey God. But so often I have neglected the Holy Spirit and forgotten to follow the Spirit. Even though I have prayed to be led, it has been out of selfish motives. I have been trying to follow Jesus all these years, but I have not been relying on the Holy Spirit. I tend to rely on myself too much and try to figure everything out, instead of relying on the Spirit. I have gotten a glimpse of what this means. The Holy Spirit is powerful; it is God's Spirit given to us. I think it takes a commitment to follow the Spirit, as it does to follow Christ. It comes down to a choice. We don't have to follow the Spirit; we don't have to rely on the Holy Spirit to guide us. He doesn't force us. So, to be led, we have to follow.

There is a cost to following the Spirit. It's called death to self, but being alive in Christ is the result. I learned something today. I have made my decision. How about you?

I so wanted to write more on this and mentioned that I would. I am feeling led by the Spirit to stop here. You can look at the scriptures about the Holy Spirit yourself if you don't already know them. All I know is that the Holy Spirit helps me in times when nothing else can. You can't make it in this life without the Holy Spirit. People will fail you; you will fail in your own strength, but God's Holy Spirit will not fail you. The Comforter, the Helper is what you need. When you need an attitude change, when you need faith, when you need help, you need the Holy Spirit.

So right now, if you want to, raise your hands, and let the fire of God consume you. Fire yourself up by letting the Holy Spirit fill you, like a gas tank being filled to the top so that there is no emptiness in the tank. So that you can be filled by Christ's Spirit himself, and nothing else. Be filled.

"Lord, I don't want anything else, but the fullness of your Spirit."

Let this prayer be yours also, that he would fill you and lead you by His Spirit.

8

HUMILITY IS ESSENTIAL

For all those who exalt themselves will be humbled, and those who humble themselves will be exalted." Luke 14:11

Humility is lowering yourself, to bring yourself to a low position. It is kind of the opposite of selfishness. If you are purposefully being selfish, you are most likely not being humble. Webster's says it means to be "not proud or haughty". I would say it is not thinking more highly of yourself than you should. Webster's defines humility as "the state or quality of being humble; freedom from **pride** and arrogance; lowliness of mind; a modest estimate of one's own worth; a sense of one's own unworthiness through imperfection and sinfulness; self-abasement; humbleness".

Freedom from pride is being humble. Pride can be tricky, and you can have pride that is good and pride that is bad. There is a fine line to meaning of it. You can be proud of others and proud of yourself for good reasons, honorable reasons. But when your pride is in yourself, and you lift yourself up because of those honorable reasons, then pride becomes very dangerous. When the praise for what you did goes beyond the fact that it honors God or helps others and starts focusing on you, then you have pride for the wrong reasons. This kind of pride is called self-righteousness. If you are right about something or living righteous, it really is to no credit to you. You are right because it is the truth, not because you are superior. You live a righteous life because that is what God's will is; you have no reason to go beyond that, and if you do, it is self-righteousness. Having this kind of pride (not being humble) is one of the most harmful and dangerous sins that will bring unwanted consequences on yourself and those around you. Selfish pride causes great harm to yourself and to the world around you. In opposition, being humble can bring about great consequences in your life and world and result in true revival. Great revivals in history come when people humble themselves; in fact, it is a promise of God.

> *"If my people, who are called by my name, will humble themselves and pray and seek my face and turn from their wicked ways, then I will hear from heaven, and I will forgive their sin and will heal their land."* 2 Chronicles 7:14

Humble yourself, or you will be humbled by God. Many have been in history, and many will be in the end. People who exalt themselves as higher than God, or smarter than God and go their own way, as if they were above all, end up being humbled in the end. It is better to humble yourself and remain humble than to get humbled by far. Revival doesn't happen to the arrogant; it happens when we humble ourselves before God.

Spencer Steak

I recall a lesson I learned about humility back when I was about eighteen. It was the 70's, and my family was in between homes since we had moved to a new area in California; Orange County to the Mountains. We were living in a camp trailer in a trailer park until they purchased some land. It was crowded, and we didn't have a lot of money that I knew of.

I had just gotten paid from one of my early jobs and wanted to celebrate and reward myself. After cashing my check, I went to the grocery store and bought myself a nice, big, fat, Spencer Steak.

Spencer Steaks are a great, flavorful cut of meat, also known today as a rib-eye. We knew that a Spencer Steak was one of the best and the most delicious; it was also expensive, just as good cuts of steak are expensive today; this meant that they were rare in our household. I took my steak home and showed it to everyone and was very proud of my great steak. I proceeded to the fire pit outside and attempted to cook my steak, which I had never done before. At first, it didn't seem to be cooking, so I got the fire hotter. It still wasn't cooking on the inside, so I cooked it longer. It ended up getting burnt on the outside and raw on the inside. I ended up with a charred, black thing with red inside. It was inedible. I was so disappointed that I had ruined the steak and had wasted the money, and I was still hungry. I threw it in the trash in front of everyone. I has very mad at myself and frustrated, but soon I started realizing how selfish I had been. It had never crossed my mind that my parents or sister might be hungry; it never occurred to me to share it. I was going to selfishly eat this delicious steak in front of my family while they had nothing. I was so prideful in the fact that I could purchase a fancy steak and thought I deserved it, that I forgot about others. I still feel bad about that today, that I was that selfish. My pride sent me to bed hungry that night. My mom offered me food, but I felt so bad and mad at myself that I couldn't eat. I did find out how not being humble can cause you heartache and, in this case, a stomachache.

My Bird Theory

One day while eating lunch, I observed some sparrows that were trying to get some food left in a dumpster. It occurred to me that they don't work jobs; they don't try to promote themselves; they just do what a bird does: fly, sing and eat. They trust God to feed them and take care of them. In response, you can hear them singing away in the trees. In fact, I just took a break outside and can hear them singing, all different types of birds. It sounds like they are praising God. Birds are everywhere due to their God-

given ability to fly, yet you don't always notice them. Some scientists estimate that there are 200 billion to 400 billion birds in the world, compared to the 7.5 billion humans; they out number us greatly. The Bible even says that God notices when a bird dies in Matthew 10:29-31:

> *"Are not two sparrows sold for a cent? And yet not one of them will fall to the ground apart from your Father. But the very hairs of your head are all numbered. So do not fear; you are more valuable than many sparrows."*

More valuable to God than the birds, we are, Yoda would say. Yet do we trust him? Do we sing our songs to Him? Do we fly with the life He has given us? Or do we somehow think that we are in control of the universe, that everything revolves around us? With what we have been given: this life, our food, our experiences, our world, all of the beautiful creation; shouldn't we be humble and lower ourselves and respect and honor our Creator?

So, my theory is that we should be like birds; humbly appreciate the food we get, the air we breathe, and should use our lives to glorify him and soar as high as we can. And use our voices to praise him with our life songs.

Speaking of songs, recently I was just privileged to see the amazing guitar player/ singer songwriter, Phil Keaggy. If you have never heard of him, you should check him out. He has been playing guitar for decades, with over 50 solo albums on his own, but many other with other artists and bands. He is considered to be in the top 5 guitarists in the world; some say he is the best. What is outstanding about Phil besides his incredible mastery of the guitar and performing ability is his humble demeanor. He exudes a joy and humility, and at the same time mesmerizes the listeners with his skill. It is not like any performer I have seen before. Phil understands that God has given him the gift to play and sing and humbly shares his life with others. Many of us have seen successful people, and there is a big difference in a humble person and a brash, prideful one. The prideful ones usually don't make it very long, or they finally realize that it is not all about them, but others, and become humble.

Jesus came to give all, not to get. He was on a mission to teach us His ways, and to die in our place, to take our punishment for our sins. We owe all to Him. We should strive to make Him popular, not ourselves. When we have a humble attitude and one that is out to serve others, God exalts us and rewards us, but all the glory goes to Him. We need to live in humility, not putting ourselves down, but doing our best every day because of what He has given us, life.

"And He died for all, that those who live should no longer live for themselves but for Him who died for them and was raised again." 2 Corinthians 5:15

Death is Essential. Die to self. Jesus came to serve, not be served. Matthew 20:28, Mark 10:45

I had to fit this in and this seems to be the place. Because to live, you have to die. Humility is the essence of dying; it takes humility to die to selfish desires. Death causes sadness, loss and pain, but is an essential part of life. For life to come forth, there has to be a dying of the old. Plants in all their beauty die, so a seed can come forth and bring life again. It is constant, like the seasons. We must continually die to our selfishness. Jesus said in Matthew 16:34 *"Whoever wants to be my disciple must deny themselves and take up their cross and follow me."* Paul also explains this in Galatians 2:20 and 5:24. Being a Christian is dying to your old nature and being born again; baptism is a symbol of that death of the old nature and resurrection of a new creation. Romans 6:4-8. It was also recorded in Luke 9:23 where Jesus said: *"Then He said to them all, 'If any want to become my followers, let them deny themselves and take up their cross daily and follow me.'"* Notice that He says take it up daily. We must choose to deny ourselves and die daily, if we truly want to follow Jesus and live in His power. As humans, it is easy for us to slip back into the habits of the old nature; it is imperative that we die daily to continue to grow in Christ.

I employ you to die. For the log to cause a flame, it needs to be burned up. Let the life of God burn in you, so that selfishness is burned to death.

Philippians 2:1-8 tells it like it is:

Therefore, if you have any encouragement from being united with Christ, if any comfort from His love, if any common sharing in the Spirit, if any tenderness and compassion, then make my joy complete by being likeminded, having the same love, being one in spirit and of one mind. Do nothing out of selfish ambition or vain conceit. Rather, in humility value others above yourselves, not looking to your own interests but each of you to the interests of the others. In your relationships with one another, have the same mindset as Christ Jesus: Who, being in very nature God, did not consider equality with God something to be used to his own advantage; rather, he made himself nothing by taking the very nature of a servant, being made in human likeness. And being found in appearance as a man, he humbled himself by becoming obedient to death—even death on a cross!"

9

RISE UP AND STEP UP

Discipline yourself to be the best, even if you are not the best. You must want it more than anyone else does. You can't just go with the flow anymore. You just don't want to fit in and do what everyone else is doing. To walk a fully alive life, you have to be the trend setter; you have to be the one that does the hard work; the one that is willing to do what it takes, not just in words but in actions. You have to do what it takes to be where you want and where God wants you. While others sit back and criticize you because you are different, they are the ones that are going to miss the revived life. You cannot let people and their opinions hold you back. You cannot let hard tasks or things that seem impossible hold you down. Do not become complacent in your life to where you are happy with the status quo. You know there is more. You have to make a conscious effort to rise up, rise up out of the common. Out of the despair, out of the rut, pull yourself out and up and start heading to the mountaintop, and don't let anything stop you!

Get Out of the Bog Now

People tend to let things bog them down and end up going nowhere. Whether it is losing weight, getting in shape, cleaning the house, writing a paper, doing a dirty job that needs to be done, or mending a relationship. Whatever it is that is always weighing on you, and you want to put off till later because it is hard or seems impossible.

Get organized, get a plan, and start doing the things you need to do. Make a list of the things that are hanging over your head and do them. Not just the physical things, but the spiritual also. The latter seems to be the hardest for all of us to do consistently, or we would all be doing amazing things for the kingdom of God. On your TO DO list, take the hardest one that you have been putting off and don't sleep until you tackle it. Tackling the giant will make the war and your progress go much smoother and quicker, just like when David defeated Goliath. The giant had stepped out for 40 days and taunted Israel. David decided to end this problem and approached Goliath, even though others would not. He then ran to the frontline and killed the giant. As soon as that big, weighty problem was gone, the Philistine army retreated and Israel was able to defeat them and plunder them. The giant was like a dam that was blocking the river. We need to unclog our pipes, and remove the thing that holds back the flow. Victory comes when we tackle and remove the hard things off our list. Revival happens when we rise up and do what needs to be done.

Volunteer for God to Use You

Just as David volunteered to do a job that others were not willing to do, we need to take some steps of faith, to volunteer. We cannot expect to have a revived life of faith if we never rise up, if we never volunteer. Maybe it's time to volunteer to do something that no one else is willing to do. Staying in the back of the pack will not bring you to the finish line as the winner.

Motor Boat

I once heard that your life can be like a motor boat. If the engine is running, it is easy to direct. If you don't get the engine running, the boat will go nowhere. It is your responsibility to get the engine running, to make the effort, to get in, to prepare for the trip, to push the gas pedal. If you are not even willing to do that, it is hard for the boat to get where it needs to be. So, do what you are supposed to do and leave the directing and results to God. So, pull the rope, crank over the engine, fire it up, get in the seat, put it in drive, press the throttle down, and let God direct you.

Put Yourself in Positions That Force You to Grow.

Peter and the Boat

One of my favorite stories in the Bible was preached to the congregation by Pastor Roy McKain, who was pastor of Christian Life Fellowship in Mayville, Wisconsin. He would preach this message at least every couple of years and said it was one of his favorites. It became one of mine, and I will never forget the impact and lesson from this story in the Bible.

I call it Peter and the boat, but it is better known as the story where Jesus walked on the water and is found in Matthew 14:22-34:

Jesus Walks on the Water

[22] Immediately Jesus made the disciples get into the boat and go on ahead of him to the other side, while he dismissed the crowd. [23] After he had

dismissed them, he went up on a mountainside by himself to pray. Later that night, he was there alone, [24] and the boat was already a considerable distance from land, buffeted by the waves because the wind was against it.

[25] Shortly before dawn Jesus went out to them, walking on the lake. [26] When the disciples saw him walking on the lake, they were terrified. 'It's a ghost,' they said, and cried out in fear.

[27] But Jesus immediately said to them: 'Take courage! It is I. Don't be afraid.'

[28] 'Lord, if it's you,' Peter replied, 'tell me to come to you on the water.' [29] 'Come,' he said.

Then Peter got down out of the boat, walked on the water and came toward Jesus. [30] But when he saw the wind, he was afraid and, beginning to sink, cried out, 'Lord, save me!'

[31] Immediately Jesus reached out his hand and caught him. 'You of little faith,' he said, 'why did you doubt?'

[32] And when they climbed into the boat, the wind died down. [33] Then those who were in the boat worshiped him, saying, 'Truly you are the Son of God.'"

There are so many applications to life in these passages. The fact that after Jesus was alone and in prayer before He walks on water through a storm to the boat, might give us a lesson on prayer and being prepared before we go out to save others. The disciples had got in the boat and were obedient and went where Jesus told them, but when they were facing opposition from the wind and waves, that's when Jesus shows up. They were scared and thought He was a ghost, but Jesus assures them it is He, so Peter says tell me to come to you. This is like, ok God, I know it is scary but I will come if you tell me to. Peter takes courage and steps out, but his faith fails when he looks at circumstances. But Jesus reaches out and catches him, and gets him back to the boat. Cool story; we can trust in Jesus to save us when we step out. Peter was the only one on earth besides Jesus that ever walked on the water. Amazing, showing us that you can do anything if God calls you to it. But that wasn't the biggest lesson. The one that really impacted me, the one lesson that haunts me about this story. It's this... there were eleven men sitting in the boat that never got up, never called to Jesus to come to Him. They worshipped Him after they saw what happened, but they were not willing to step out. I don't want to be one of the eleven; I don't want you to be one of the eleven who did not get to walk on the water. I don't want you to be one of the eleven who did not get to be pulled up by Jesus and brought back to the boat. Wouldn't you rather be Peter, who got to walk on water with Jesus? In life, you can sit there and watch or you can ask God to allow you to step out. It doesn't matter what type of personality you have, anyone could have stepped out of that boat. I pray to God that I won't be one of the eleven in life. I pray that you won't be one of the eleven. I pray that you will step out, in the face of opposition, even though no one else does, and experience the relationship with Jesus, doing His will and getting to do supernatural things that only God can allow you to get through. Don't just sit in the boat. I pray that you step up and step out.

10

THE BIG 3 + 1

The big three plus one, are probably the most meaningful to me in having a revived life and are a foundation that every Christian needs to have to do God's will. These three plus one, are the bread and butter of the Christian walk of faith. The big three came to me while when I was spending the day at High Cliff Park, preparing for a sermon that I had to preach at the church where I was filling in for the pastor. I wanted to really hear from God on what message I should share with the congregation. As I prayed and asked for His help, I was prompted to read in Psalms, and these principles jumped out at me and into an outline form. They were principles that had been drilled into me all through my Christian life, but I had never seen them and never realized that they were so important to God that He would show me that if I should preach on anything, it should be these three. On top of that, the big three are principles that we should never go without, be without or stop doing. When it comes to being revived, I believe you have to get the big three down before you can go anywhere or do anything. The big three should never leave you, and should never be missing from your life. The sermon was called "Being balanced in an unbalanced world." If you want to minister to others and to have a strong walk with God, you need these three big essentials in your life. You can live without them, but you will not be very effective in your faith without them. Two of them are very well known, and you hear them emphasized over and over, but they can never be overlooked or forgotten. The plus one was added to this list later, when I learned a very valuable lesson that I will go over at the end of this chapter. We need to be reminded of them again and again until they are a part of our lives. Let's look at Psalms to see what the big three are as I rediscovered them again that day at High Cliff.

#1 of the Big Three

The first of the big three is really a choice on your part to listen to and follow God. It is initiated by God when He calls you. In John 6:44 Jesus says *"No one can come to me unless the Father who sent me draws them, and I will raise them up at the last day."* We are **all** drawn to God by the Father, and we know from scripture that **He draws all people to himself** (John 12:32) through the death and resurrection of His Son. While the second and third of the big three and the plus one, are choices, they are really spiritual disciplines that we need to choose to do. This first one of the big three though, is a heart response that brings us into a right relationship with God. The first of the big three is found in Psalm 51 verse 12: *"Restore to me the joy of your salvation and grant me a willing spirit, to sustain me."*

#1: A Willing Spirit

Willingness is what we need if we want to be sustained in this world. When we lose our willingness, we lose our sustainment. If you know the story of Jonah and the big fish in the Book of Jonah, you see that Jonah was called by God to preach to the wicked city of Nineveh. He chose to run from God, and he and those around him suffered the consequences. God gave him another chance, and when he finally obeyed, the king of Nineveh and the whole city repented and turned to God for forgiveness.

Psalm 51 was written when the prophet, Nathan, had confronted David of committing adultery with Bathsheba and killing her husband. David was asking God for that willingness again to follow Him. He was asking forgiveness and breaking before God. He knew he was wrong in what he did. We have all been unwilling to do God's will, and we need to ask him for that willingness and to create a clean heart in us. Only God can forgive us; we need to be willing to ask him for help. God requires faithfulness on our part. Verse 12, *"truth in the inner parts,"* one version says. Verse 17 says "*My sacrifice, O God, is a broken spirit; a broken and contrite heart you, God, will not despise.*" God will restore us when we confess and repent before Him and choose to do His will instead of our own. The result of a willing spirit is found in Psalm 51:13 "*Then I will teach transgressors your ways so that sinners will turn back to you.*" You can only be effective in ministry if you have a willing spirit. You can only be effective in your faith if you have a willing spirit; you can only experience inner revival if you have a willing spirit.

Here are a couple more passages to think about:

"This is the message we have heard from him and proclaim to you, that God is light, and in Him is no darkness at all. If we say we have fellowship with Him while we walk in darkness, we lie and do not practice the truth. But if we walk in the light, as He is in the light, we have fellowship with one another, and the blood of Jesus His Son cleanses us from all sin. If we say we have no sin, we deceive ourselves, and the truth is not in us. If we confess our sins, He is faithful and just to forgive us our sins and to cleanse us from all unrighteousness. If we say we have not sinned, we make Him a liar, and His word is not in us. My little children, I am writing these things to you so that you may not sin. But if anyone does sin, we have an advocate with the Father, Jesus Christ the righteous. He is the propitiation for our sins, and not for ours only but also for the sins of the whole world." 1 John 1:5 - 2:2

*"Be shepherds of God's flock that is under your care, watching over them— not because you must, **but because you are willing**, as God wants you to be; not pursuing dishonest gain, but eager to serve; ³ not lording it over those entrusted to you, but being examples to the flock."* 1 Peter 5:2-3

#2 of the Big Three

If you jump a little bit over in psalms to Psalm 55:22, you will see the second of the Big Three that I noticed in these chapters.

"Cast your cares on the Lord and he will sustain you."

The Hebrew word for cast, "Shaw-lak," means to throw out, throw down, or away. In Luke 19:35 Jesus' Triumphal entry, the people *cast* their garments on the donkey and the road. We should let Jesus sit on our burdens and trample them. And in 1 Peter 5:7 we are told to *"Cast all your anxiety on him because he cares for you."* We give our anxieties, our cares our burdens to God by casting them to him through prayer. That's the second principle in the Big Three.

#2 Is being a person of Prayer.

Prayer is essential if you want to keep your faith alive and keep your relationship with God right. Prayer is a hard discipline that many of us struggle with. It is simply just taking time to talk and listen to God. We get so busy that we forget to do this on a daily basis. Most people pray when they get in trouble or feel they have no other option, but prayer should be ongoing and helps us to be closer to God. But it really takes a conscious decision and takes much discipline to make it a habit in our lives. It may take many, many years to develop a consistent prayer life, but it is invaluable and will bring such great rewards and peace. I have seen God answer so many prayers in my life, some answers took years, some were instant, some seemed impossible, but God is all powerful and can do anything. We are told not to give up by Jesus in Luke 18:1-8, to pray without ceasing in 1 Thessalonians 5:17 and in Philippians 4:6-7 to *"_Be anxious for nothing, but in everything by prayer and supplication, with thanksgiving, let your requests be made known to God; and the peace of God, which surpasses all understanding, will guard your hearts and minds through Christ Jesus."*

A simple, good way to start at being consistent in prayer, I learned from a pastor. He said to just list five people who need God in their lives and pray for them every day. It only took me seconds a day to do this and helped me to pray every day. They were people I worked with and were easy to pray for when I got up or before I walked into work. After doing that for a long time, it developed into a larger list. First of all, I pray for my immediate family, then my extended family list, then my list of people I know in the workplace. It still only takes a minute or two, but helps me to pray. I then can pray about other things or interject prayers as things come to mind. It is an easy way for me to be consistent. And of course, I don't just stick to my little list. I try to pray throughout the day and keep the conversation between me and God going, which is easy to forget also, but we should be in constant prayer throughout our days and lives. We need to rely on God, and He should be the one we are going to all day long with our requests, our concerns and our questions.

God does answer prayers, I have seen him change people right before my eyes, and I have seen him answer prayers and change hearts that took 25 years. Some answers we may never see, but it is our job to pray; it is God's job to answer. If we don't ask, we can't expect an answer.

If you want peace in your life; if you want a vibrant life, full of faith; if you want to see the world changed and people changed, have you asked God? Prayer is one of the big ones; don't expect to see revival if you don't pray.

"Nothing will be impossible in your family, life, and world if you are a person of prayer." Pastor Roy McKain

#3 of the Big Three

Psalm 56:4 David wrote this: *"In God, whose word I praise—in God I trust and am not afraid. What can mere mortals do to me?"* David praised God's word. He loved it. We should also. Praise means to be foolish about it, to rave about it, to boast about it.

#3 of the Big Three is being a person of the Word.

As a Christian, this has been ingrained into us, and it should be. We need to read our bibles; we need to meditate on God's Word; we need to know what God's thoughts are toward us. These are not just words written by men, but they are words God had men write down, in fact, at least 40 different men, over thousands of years, to bring one message to mankind. There are a lot of verses on the word of God, here are just a few:

> "All Scripture is God-breathed and is useful for teaching, rebuking, correcting and training in righteousness, so that the servant of God may be thoroughly equipped for every good work." 2 Timothy 3:16-17

> "This is what we speak, not in words taught us by human wisdom but in words taught by the Spirit, explaining spiritual realities with Spirit-taught words." 1 Corinthians 2:13

> "Jesus answered, 'It is written: 'Man shall not live on bread alone, but on every word that comes from the mouth of God.'" Matthew 4:4

> "For prophecy never had its origin in the human will, but prophets, though human, spoke from God as they were carried along by the Holy Spirit." 1 Peter 1:21

> "For the word of God is alive and active. Sharper than any double-edged sword, it penetrates even to dividing soul and spirit, joints and marrow; it judges the thoughts and attitudes of the heart." Hebrews 4:12

I am reminded again of the dream I had about the stranger in black, who flung his knives into my back. After that dream, later that week, I read these verses in Ephesians 6:16-17:

> "In addition to all, taking up the shield of faith with which you will be able to extinguish all the flaming arrows of the evil one. And take the helmet of salvation, and the sword of the Spirit, which is the word of God."

What I needed in the dream was the shield of faith and the word of God which is like a sword to defend myself. We need weapons to fight spiritual attacks as well, and the word of God is like a sword and is what Jesus used when he was tempted in Matthew 4:1-11.

Without the word of God, we are defenseless. Even our prayers will not work if we ignore God's word. Proverbs 28:9

If you love God, you will love his word, and you will spend time reading it daily. You will not know the power of revival if you do not know God's word. Knowing about it is one thing, living and obeying it is another.

So those are the three. The two you have heard over and over - the word and prayer, prayer and the word; however you remember them, remember and do them. Be a person of prayer, a person of the word and have a willing heart toward God.

You cannot get by without these three. Yes, you may fail, and like I said in Chapter two, even if it takes how many years? Seventy. Don't move on if you aren't committed to these three. Do not pass go, do not collect anything, go to jail and don't try to get out unless you do it with these three, and they become a life principle that is practiced and applied daily.

Plus One

The Plus one is adding one to yourself. Doing your life with others is very important. Fellowship is the plus one that we need to make choices about and make sure we are not left alone. Jesus had the twelve; we need people around us. Fellowship is an important principle and is key to being personally revived and seeing others revived.

The Danger of Not Being in Fellowship

A friend of mine I used to go to church with, stopped going and did his own home Bible studies. He got into a doctrine that seemed to make sense, it was very subtle. In the end, he was convinced all Christians were wrong; all the songs we sing are wrong and the church was going astray, but the doctrine he was believing in was twisted and was saying things scripture did not. He was clearly in a cult, believing one man who taught this doctrine. The cult he fell into was called the Shepherd's Chapel. Run from this teaching because it looks good on outside, but is clearly demonic. This really made an impact on me to see how easily people can be deceived. It also taught me a great lesson, that there is safety in numbers. The devil wants so dearly to separate us from the church, once we are isolated, he can have a hay-day with us. Since then, I make sure I do not fall into the trap of thinking I know better than other Christians. At the same time that I was researching my friend's claims, I found another cult that Christians had adopted hook, line, and sinker: The Weigh Down Workshop. Thousands of Christians read the book that was supposed be a Biblical way to lose weight, but the leader went too far and said her way was the only way, and her church the only church, and had people telling off their pastors and that they were all wrong. I read the accounts of people that were deceived in this cult and had realized they were deceived and had to go back to their pastors and apologize for acting like that and for falling for such non-sense. 1 Timothy 4:1 tells us: "*The Spirit clearly says that in later times some will abandon the faith and follow deceiving spirits and things taught by demons.*" I hear so many people say "I don't believe in organized religion." What they are really saying is that they have their own beliefs, and they don't want to follow God's plan. It is very dangerous to not be around other believers, and there are great benefits to being around others.

If you want to stay sharp, you need to be around other Christians. (Proverbs 27:17 "*As iron sharpens iron, so one person sharpens another.*") Other Christians will inspire you, keep you in check, challenge you, and serve as an example to you. They can pray for you and be there when you need help. The Lone Ranger had Tonto. Ecclesiastes 4:9-12 says:

> "*Two are better than one, because they have a good return for their labor: If either of them falls down, one can help the other up. But pity anyone who falls and has no one to help them up. Also, if two lie down together, they will keep warm. But how can one keep warm alone? Though one may be overpowered, two can defend themselves. A cord of three strands is not quickly broken.*"

Mentor and be mentored; you will never get mentored by staying alone and being separated from the body. To learn from others, we have to actively be around them, we have to make friends and be a friend. We learn from each other. Jesus taught the twelve by being with them. Fellowship is important; it was in the early church, and it is just as important today.

> "And let us consider how we may spur one another on toward love and good deeds, not giving up meeting together, as some are in the habit of doing, but encouraging one another—and all the more as you see the Day approaching." Hebrews 10:24-25

So, you need to choose to be involved with others if you really want to live to the fullest. Maybe you have isolated yourself from others for one reason or another. You need to get involved with God's people, visit a church, join a Bible study or group, like a men's or women's group, a youth group, a college and career group, a singles or married group. Get to know others in the church; you will be better for it. Force yourself to connect to the right people; people that will help you grow and people who will not keep you in mediocrity.

The three plus one, are vital to your Christian walk, and you need to cultivate and practice these. I can't imagine that they will not promote revival.

11

SERVE GOD COMPLETELY

Recently, I heard the famous comedian and actor, Bill Murray, quote this statement in an interview **"This is not a dress rehearsal, this is your life."** [1] He was talking about giving it all
in work and in life, which most likely has contributed to his success as an actor, comedian and human being. There's no do-overs, so we better get it right in this life. There will be no other chance we get than now. "This is not a dress rehearsal" has been quoted by many people, and we don't know exactly who first said it; it did show up in a newspaper though, in 1953. It was in the Covina Argus-Citizen newspaper of Covina, California. Pastor Lawrence T Holman titled his evening sermon: "Life is not a dress rehearsal." [2] It was interesting looking back at old newspapers that they included the titles to sermons back then, and some even preached a little in their ads. But most interesting of all is how profound this statement is. So many times, we take life for granted. So many of us casually go through life, just taking what is handed out, instead of actively living it and giving our all. You will never accomplish anything worthwhile

---

Notes:

[1] Interview with Charlie Rose Feb. 11th 2014 Hulu

[2] 1953 May 7, Covina Argus-Citizen, Section II, Quote Page 6, Column 3, Your Church Invites You, (Schedule of Church of the Nazarene, Location: First and College, Pastor: Lawrence T. Holman), Covina, California. (Newspaper Archive)

if you only give a little effort, if you are living partially for the Lord. You have to have the attitude that every day is the real thing; it is your life. You can either waste your time by goofing around and not taking life seriously, or you can give 100% to your audience. Shakespeare said "All the world's a stage." In a way, it really is. How we act and live our lives is played out before God and others. How we live can greatly impact those around us for good or bad. Most importantly, how we live impacts our relationship with God. We have to be open to God and what he wants us to do. One preacher said this simple prayer every day as he woke up and looked in the mirror "Good Morning, Lord! What do you have planned for me? I want to be part of it." Another preacher said we should wake up every day and say, " Here I am, Lord. What do you want me to do?" We should be living our lives to please Him, so we should find out what pleases Him, what his will is, and then do it and live it. 100%

> *"For you were once darkness, but now you are light in the Lord. Live as children of light (for the fruit of the light consists in all goodness, righteousness and truth) and find out what pleases the Lord." Ephesians 5:8-10*

> *"Do not conform to the pattern of this world, but be transformed by the renewing of your mind. Then you will be able to test and approve what God's will is—his good, pleasing and perfect will". Romans 12:2*

> *"So that you may live a life worthy of the Lord and please him in every way: bearing fruit in every good work, growing in the knowledge of God" Colossians 1:10*

While writing this, I am convicted and do have regrets on the times I have wasted time doing wrong things or doing nothing at all. There are many times in our days and in life that we need rest and recouping, but we forget, I think a lot, of how important our life is. It is not just an act; this is the real thing. Why not make the most of it? I will be talking more about this in the final chapter of this book, but here I want to explore a person from the Bible who stands out and who lived 100% completely for God. His name was Josiah.

Completely or Partially?

You can read the story of King Josiah in 2 Kings chapter 22 and 23, and also in 2 Chronicles 34 and 35. He was the last good King of Judah to rule in the Southern Kingdom of Israel. His Father, Amon, was wicked, and so was his Grandfather, Manasseh, 2 Kings 21:20. In spite of his wicked examples, he was able to live a life for God that changed things in his time. Who knows, his mother could have been the influence of his faith, or maybe Jeremiah and/or other prophets who were around at his time. During his life, he repaired the temple, removed **all** the detestable idols, got everyone to follow the Lord and had them observe the Passover. 2 Kings 22:2 says *"He did what was right in the eyes of the Lord and followed **completely** the ways of his father David, not turning aside to the right or to the left."* There's that word completely, which also means all. When the book of the law was found, telling of God's judgment on Israel, this is how he responded: 22:19 says *"Because your heart was responsive and you humbled yourself"* God heard him and did not allow him to see the destruction of Israel. Even though he died in battle, he went down completely sold out to God. While he lived, he lived completely; he gave it all to God. Even though he could not change the history of the coming judgment on Israel, he did what was right in his time, completely.

This is really interesting, the fact that he did experience a revival, an awakening to God, and the people turned to God and removed wickedness. There was a restoration while he lived. But the most interesting thing to note was that he was alive to God. He did what was right himself, which is really the premise of this book. If we want to see revival, if we want to see people turn to God wholly, then we need to follow God wholly and completely. No matter what the world says, no matter what is going to happen, we have to live for God. Think about what

Josiah's life would have been, if he only partially followed God, or partially obeyed the law, or partially tore down the idols. His legacy would have been that he was a partially good king and partially served God. Why would anyone ever want that as their legacy? He partially lived. Yet so many of us do. We give a little to God or a portion to God, we partially obey. What does that get us? We all fail God, but this should not stop us from giving all. Maybe up to this point in your life, you have only given partially. Why not ask God to help you give all and just do it. You may find out by doing that, that your life will leave an amazing legacy like Josiah's did. You have one life, don't do it partially. Live it fully.

> *"Neither before nor after Josiah was there a king like him who turned to the Lord as he did- with all his heart and with all his soul and with all his strength, in accordance with all the law of Moses." 2 Kings 23:25*

In a Relationship

While at our men's group at church, a statement like this was made comparing our relationship with God like that of our spouse... "If we treated our spouse like we treat God, we would be divorced." In a relationship, you have to spend time with the other person; you have to love the other person, and you have to trust the other person. We give our all to our spouse and loved ones, but don't give our all to God. I thought to myself about it and thought wow, I don't really give my all to my spouse either. Then I thought, does anyone really give 100% to the ones they love, or do we hold back a little. We may hold back because of past hurts we received from the other person, or we know their limitations to love us back so we don't give all. Oh, we say we do give all, but do we really? You have heard people say "I will never trust anyone again after what they did to me." or "I will never fully give my heart to someone, you just can't trust them." It is hard for us to give our whole heart after it has been broken by someone or abused, taken for granted, or treated with disloyalty. So, we hold back and part of that is so that we don't get hurt again by people. Sometimes our heart is damaged and needs to heal before we can trust someone again.

With God it is different though. He can be fully trusted. He is always loyal, always honest, always good. He will never leave us or forsake us.

We should not look at Him the same we do as people. Even though we are told in 1 John 4:20 *"For whoever does not love their brother and sister, whom they have seen, cannot love God, whom they have not seen."* We should love people and are commanded to. His love is different than ours; His love is perfect. That's why we can love people, because of His love that He gives us. His love gives us hope to love others, even though we may not be able to trust people. We can love them, if we have put our full trust in Him. In God, we can trust with our hearts and give all, but we hold back and wonder why we are not complete. You will be complete and revived when you are fully trusting that God loves you completely, and that the Holy Spirit is stronger than anyone, any sin or anything that would keep you from Him and makes you complete. There has to be resolve in your heart that you are going to trust God completely, no matter what happens, no matter how hard you may fall. You are going to trust Him, obey Him, and do His will completely. I guess to sum it up, you have to fully trust God 100%.

There Has to Be a Turning

In a relationship, there has to be a turning back if it is to be kept alive. We cannot just say we are flawed and will mess up and leave it to that. There seems to be a problem in churches today where Christians have this attitude. They over-emphasize the fact that we are sinners, that we will fall short. The problem with that is that we just stay there in sin; we know we will sin and that we are but human, so we live in that instead of turning to God. Or maybe we have turned to God at one time, but we have failed, so we stay there and stay away from God instead of turning to him. There has to be a turning back to God personally. If you look at the previous verse about Josiah, you will see it says "*Neither before nor after Josiah was there a king like him who **turned to the Lord** as he did.*" There has to be a turning, if there is going to be revival. That turning is what we call repentance. Repentance is a word people don't seem to like today. But it basically means "to turn." Turning from not following God, to following Him.

Revival Requires Repentance

There has to be a turning to God from our sin; that is repentance and is necessary for a true relationship as it is for revival. There has never been a change in a person without there being a turning first. There also has never been a revival on a large scale without repentance. The people must be sorrowful for their sin and turn from it and turn to God. So, it is with Inner Revival. If you want to be fully alive to God and fully accomplish His will, then you need to be sorrowful for your sin and turn from it to God. Your attitude of your heart must be sorrowful for any sin in your life, and you must actively turn from it and turn to God's ways. Notice how Josiah responded in 2 Kings 22:19, when Josiah heard what God had spoken about the sins of Israel: "*You tore your robes and wept in my presence.*" He had an utter disgust and grief for the sins that Israel committed by serving other gods. His grief came from finding out what God was going to do because of this sin. What the sin had caused. Tearing of clothes was how they showed deep grief and sorrow. I would say it was a symbol on the outside of how they felt inside. The prophet Joel said "*Rend your heart and not your garments. Return to the LORD your God, for He is gracious and compassionate, slow to anger and abounding in love, and He relents from sending calamity.*" Joel 2:13 Do you have this kind of grief over your sin or your nation's sin? Does it make you want to tear/rend something, then rend your heart? Repentance should cause this in you. When you realize what sin has done to you and others and how it affects your relationship with God, it is enough to make you grieve and weep. God created us with emotions; sin should cause a response of sorrow and grief that brings us to tears. It is a response from the heart; emotions show the condition of our hearts.

Revival Requires Forgiveness

You need to find out what's stopping you from giving your all in your relationship with God and change that. Once we repent and turn to God, He shows his forgiveness. The Bible tells us in 1 John 1:9 *"If we confess our sins, he is faithful and just and will forgive us our sins and purify us from all unrighteousness."* God is faithful and will forgive when we repent. God forgives, and the Bible tells us that we should forgive also. In fact, Jesus said *"But if you do not forgive others their sins, your Father will not forgive your sins."* Matthew 6:15

We cannot expect to see revival in our hearts and in others if we are not willing to forgive. God is willing to forgive, yet we want to hold grudges. God is willing to forgive, yet we hold on to our past and wallow in it and let it hold us back. Even though Josiah tore down the strongholds, the high places, the idols and killed the priests who practiced at the high places. He had the people celebrate the Passover. We need to accept the sacrifice Jesus made for us and others to cover their sin. In 2 Chronicles 35:7 *"Josiah provided for all the lay people who were there a total of thirty thousand lambs and goats for the Passover offerings."* Josiah did not hold a grudge against the people. He made sure they had the offering to give for the Passover. Wow! I guess what I am trying to say here is we need to celebrate the covering God has provided for our sin and others. We shouldn't look back, but celebrate God's forgiveness. We can't live in the grief forever; we have to move on. If you want to see real revival, then you have to repent and you have to forgive others and yourself, just as God does. If you don't, you won't move on, you won't ever live and die the way God wants you to.

A Final Warning
All or Nothing, Hot or Cold

In Revelations 3:16 we read these words from our Lord: "*So, because you are lukewarm--neither hot nor cold--I am about to spit you out of my mouth.*" I am not going to give examples of water temperatures here and what it means. There is a warning to us. I believe the Lord calls us to give 100% hot or cold, no in between. No partial serving of the Lord, but full out devotion. He goes on to say in verse 19 to "*be earnest and repent.*" So, we realize we are not useful to God in our current lukewarm condition, we must repent. It is a warning not to take lightly. We can either go on in our lives as if this is not for us; if his words meant nothing, or we can earnestly repent, now! The last thing I would ever want is to be spit out of the Lord's mouth and to see people spit out. It's time to repent and live.

How would it look if you were fully living for God 100%? It would mean that you could not hold anything back from him. You could not be selfish; you would have to die completely to self to do this; it must be done. There is a cost to living for God, for being revived. You must die. Die to the world; die to your own will. Die to selfishness and pride. What if you do this? What life God would give you, if you turn from selfishness to Godliness.

Fully Ripe Nectarine

Yesterday, I enjoyed eating a perfectly ripe Nectarine. It was just at the fullness of ripeness and flavor. It brought me such joy and tasted so good. It even reminded me of memories of summer. It is funny how a taste can bring back a memory or a feeling we once had. It was almost as if the goodness of this nectarine was ministering to me and giving me more than just food, but also happiness for a brief moment. Maybe your memory has been triggered by a taste or smell that reminded you of a time in your life. This nectarine was so amazing; I was cherishing the taste. I realized if that nectarine was not 100% ripe, it would have done nothing for me. If it was under ripe and sour, I would have spit it out and would have thrown it in the trash. If it was rotten, I would have done the same. But it was right where as it should be, at the maximum ripeness. I believe God is pleased when our life is right before Him, when it is where it should be. He enjoys it so much that He blesses us more than we think we could be. It's like the feeling from eating that perfectly ripe fruit; it reminds us of stuff, good stuff. Will you serve God completely? Will you experience inner revival? I hope so. I hope to see you in Heaven! Do what it takes to get right with God and maintain your relationship with Him and live completely.

12

ACTIVELY RESIST

Enter spiritual warfare. Go on the offensive; don't just wait for the enemy to attack you. Take action

Resist the devil and he will flee
Resist temptation
Resist pride
Resist the love of the world; Keep yourself from being polluted by the world
Resist the false gods. Have no other gods
Resist hate
Resist sin

Sin in your camp will hold you and others back. We all sin, but we all can be made new. We can overcome temptations. Whatever it takes, do not let sin rule. Don't accept it and justify it. Don't beat yourself up, just deal with it. Definitely don't pretend sin is not real. When you are tempted, find the way out. Ask God for the way out and keep asking him for help until you are out. A revived life is an overcoming life. The Lord has overcome the world, and He is in you, so you must have faith that He will help you conquer temptation and sin. When you recognize the temptation, it is the time to go to war.

Sin Sick

We cannot have revival if we are infected with sin. Our country is sick and dying. Many claim to believe in God in our country, but somehow we have allowed ourselves to be infected with the sin of the world. We have confused being tolerant and loving with accepting, allowing, dabbling and indulging. We have let evil reign and have not realized the disease that sin carries; it carries death. Sin always leads to death. James says this in Chapter 1:14,15:

> "But each person is tempted when they are dragged away by their own evil desire and enticed. Then, after desire has conceived, it gives birth to sin; and sin, when it is full-grown, gives birth to death."

And in the book of Romans, God's word says that the wages of sin is death. 6:23. The United States has basically allowed itself to be sickened by sin and now is dead. There is only one answer. When Christians have allowed sin in their camp and have carried on like the world and have let the sickness that infects the world infect them, it takes more than resisting; it takes repentance. We have heard the answer before in 2 Chronicles 7:14:

> "If my people, who are called by my name, will humble themselves and pray and seek my face and turn from their wicked ways, then I will hear from heaven, and I will forgive their sin and will heal their land."

We must humble ourselves before God, seek God, and turn from our wicked ways. We must actively do this; it cannot be a principle or a belief. We have to do this if we want to see God heal our land. If we want to see revival in our lives and corporately in our country, we must actively, earnestly, with everything we have, repent. We must do this;

Inner Revival

otherwise, we are just playing games and want to continue in sin and eventually will be dead.

We have to make a choice; either we are going to let sin dominate us, or we are going to resist. When we resist the devil, he flees. James tells us in James 4:7 *"Submit yourselves, then, to God. **Resist the devil, and he will flee from you.**"*

The Bible tells us he will flee if we resist. Too often we let him keep tempting us. Why would you want to give in and let the devil win? We give up too easy; we want to have the best of everything. We think we can get away with it, because we know God will forgive us. The devil knows this too, and he will persist until he has us. And everyone knows the guilt you have to live with after you sin. The devil has labeled you a sinner, a failure, and knows he can probably get you to believe the lie that you cannot stop that sin. If you are losing a battle or have been wounded by sin, what do you do in a battle? You either fight or die. Many are living a dead life because they refuse to resist. They have done it before, but the devil keeps coming back to wear them down. There is only one way out. We have to resist. Jesus is way more powerful than Satan, and he will flee when we submit ourselves to God. He can't fight God or Christ in you, so stand and fight. Live a life of resistance to the devil! There is hope for those who feel no hope; don't let the devil keep picking you apart while you are down. It's time to rise up, time to resist, time to be a winner. You cannot lose with God.

There is Hope for the Church and America

There is hope for you, your country and even America. Even the most wicked people can turn around and seek God. Don't be afraid of evil. Don't give in and think there is no hope and just live like everyone else. Live the way Jesus wants you to. In John chapter 11 is the story of Lazarus and how Jesus brought him back to life. In verse 11, Jesus says *"Our friend Lazarus has fallen asleep; but I am going there to wake him up."* Our country may be asleep; some churches may be asleep; people are asleep. The disciples thought He was just saying Lazarus was asleep, but He then explained that He was dead.

Even though there is so much death around you, Jesus can wake up Lazarus. He can wake those around you. Do not be afraid, fear not. There are so many verses in the Bible where we are told to "fear not." We are not to fear evil, but should have a healthy fear of God. The fear of the devil is one of no hope and torture and lies. Fearing God is out of respect to the one who made us, can destroy us, but most importantly of all has the power to resurrect us from the dead. Resist any notions that God won't bring you through anything, only the devil wants to hurt you; resist him, and he has to flee.

Not fearing Satan and all the world can throw at you is a way to resist. The enemy would love to have you live in fear. The fear of what people will do; fear of past failures will keep you from having victory. We need to stop fearing failure and start believing in God's truth and strength; we need to have the right perspective of fear. We need to stop living in darkness and start shining our light. The light is Jesus. He will dispel the darkness. Resist the lies the devil tries to make you imagine.

> *"Casting down imaginations, and every high thing that exalteth itself against the knowledge of God, and bringing into captivity every thought to the obedience of Christ;" 2 Corinthians 10:5*

Don't put up with lies any more. Think about what's true.

> *"Finally, brothers and sisters, whatever is true, whatever is noble, whatever is right, whatever is pure, whatever is lovely, whatever is admirable--if anything is excellent or praiseworthy--think about such things". Philippians 4:8*

Resist evil in your mind, and then you will start doing what is right. Ask god to help you; he will.

13

THE GREATEST VIRTUE

The greatest weapon we have in this life is love. I call it a weapon because it is so powerful that nothing can stop it. Love has the ability to touch and soften the hardest of hearts. Love is a game changer. When you have genuine love, it motivates you to do things that seem impossible. It causes you to look beyond yourself and look to the needs of others. You can do things for others and not have love like 1 Corinthians 13 says, but when you are motivated by God's pure love and empowered by His love, there is nothing that can combat that.

Love Never Fails

There is a Christian worship song chorus that was popular that says...

"One thing remains
One thing remains
Your love never fails, it never gives up, it never runs out on me
Your love never fails, it never gives up, it never runs out on me Your Love
Your Love

So true that God's love never fails, never gives up, or runs out. I have experienced this in my life over and over. When faced with difficult circumstances and situations or in everyday life, in the most unexpected times, I sense God's love toward me. I may read a verse, or hear His voice speaking to my heart, whatever and however He does it, I am assured that He loves me and He is getting that across like no one else can. When everything else in this world fails, when people fail us, when systems fail us, our flesh and self-help efforts fail, God comes through with His love and transforms everything. I could not continue being a Christian if it was just a religion of rules and laws to follow. Being a Christian is a relationship, the best relationship you can have, where God himself demonstrates His love to you. I have not experienced anything greater in my whole life than His love. I have noticed that God's love does three things...

Love Changes Us

Love makes all the difference in the world and can change the world.

To be revived and stay revived, you have to have this love; God's love. If you have it, you cannot fail in this life.

We are told in the Bible to:
Walk in Love:
"And this is love: that we walk in obedience to his commands. As you have heard from the beginning, his command is that you walk in love." 2 John 1:6

"And walk in the way of love, just as Christ loved us and gave himself up for us as a fragrant offering and sacrifice to God." Eph. 5:2

We are:
Commanded to Love:

"Jesus replied: 'Love the Lord your God with all your heart and with all your soul and with all your mind.' This is the first and greatest commandment. And the second is like it: 'Love your neighbor as yourself.'" Matthew 22:37-39

We are told that:
God is Love:

And so we know and rely on the love God has for us."God is love. Whoever lives in love, lives in God, and God in them." 1 John 4:16

We are supposed to:
Add Love:

*"For this very reason, make every effort to **add** to your faith goodness; and to goodness, knowledge; and to knowledge, self-control; and to self-control, perseverance; and to perseverance, godliness; and to godliness, mutual affection; and to mutual affection, **love**." 2 Peter 1:5-7*

So, If We Are Supposed to Love God and Others, How Do We Do It?

Well that's just it, you do it by doing it. Even though love is referred to as a feeling, love is demonstrated by action, it's something you do. Or let me put it this way, because you love, you will act. For example: A young couple in love are not really in love if all they have is the feeling of love. They **do** all they can to show the other person that they love them. Love is not realized unless it is acted out. The young couple would not be in love if they never cared about each other, if they never spent time with each other, if they never reached out to each other, if they never talked to each other.

Love has a powerful way of reviving you. When you know you are loved, it changes you. I recently got a message from a relative who probably does not have long to live. The message simply said that they had always liked me. This action of speaking this into my life really made me feel loved. If the person would not have acted and spoke it, I would have never known that they cared for me. Sometimes love is expressed in words. But the words need to be backed up by action. This relative had never acted unloving toward me, so when they said the words, I knew it was true. When only words come and there is no action, there can be doubt as to if the person does love us.

It is interesting that the greatest act of love that God did for us was to send His Son to die for us, and Jesus willingly laid down His life for us. He made a major sacrifice for us, which proves His words toward us. So we love by action, by speaking, by caring, by acting, by sacrificing. It's also interesting to note that God's message and His plan of delivering it is through people. He told us to go and proclaim the good news of how God loves us. How meaningful it is, when it comes from God and through a person. No other way would we really know that he really loves us. God created us to love; what an awesome privilege it is to share His love with others. These verses seem to fit here, so take a look at them.

"Be imitators of God, therefore, as dearly love children and live a life of love, just as Christ loved us and gave himself up for us as a fragrant offering and sacrifice to God." Ephesians 5:1,2

Love is a win/win/win situation. God is loved, we are loved, people are loved.

Live to Give

I heard this phrase from a preacher years ago named Wayne Myers. "Live to Give" was his message. I have never forgotten that phrase even though I heard it back in the early 80s at Koinonia Christian fellowship in Hanford, California. It is a true statement, and I think the premise is that we should be living to give, not just financially, but giving love. It seems that the most successful people I have seen in life did live to give. Every time I have given to others unselfishly, I have found that I am the one who truly gets blessed. It's not the receiver who gets blessed, it is the giver. In the end, nothing really matters except the times when you loved someone. Things are temporal and do not reciprocate the love we all need to experience. Giving and living a life of love is the goal we should all strive to obtain in this short life. When you give love to someone else, something happens in you that can't be explained, it's what we were created to do, and we have had the example that our Creator gave. Life is so unfulfilling if we only live to get. Change your perspective now and live to give. People you have never heard of have impacted thousands, if not millions, in their lifetime living a giving lifestyle. Revival doesn't go anywhere without love. Don't stop loving, start today and live to give.

People Stop Loving for Many Reasons

It may be that they were hurt by someone. Or something didn't seem to go right for them so they decided to get bitter about it. They may have not even noticed that they have become bitter and have stopped loving, but they are not the loving person they used to be. Their motivation is not to love anymore, but to pour out hate on others and make them pay for their pain. They have become a negative person. You have seen them, maybe you have become one or at least on occasion. There is no excuse for continuing to live in bitterness and being mean and hateful to others. The root of bitterness (Heb. 12:15) has caused many to live a hellish existence on this earth and caused those around them horrific pains. Bitterness brings death; if you want to be alive, you have to destroy the root, chop it up, don't allow it to grow any longer. Bitterness is an easy trap to fall into, and before we know it, we have done so much damage in the name of hate and bitterness that it seems impossible to turn that around or do anything about it. But there is hope, and I believe it is a choice. We cannot change what has been done to us, but we can change our attitude, we can make a choice to be positive instead of negative; we can choose to forgive and love. God will heal us and help us, but we have been given freewill to choose. We can choose to go on in death or life. The Bible tells us to choose life, just as the Israelites had to in Deuteronomy 30:

" When all these blessings and curses I have set before you come on you and you take them to heart wherever the L̲o̲r̲d̲ your God disperses you among the nations, ² and when you and your children return to the L̲o̲r̲d̲ your God and obey him with all your heart and with all your soul according to everything I command you today, ³ then the L̲o̲r̲d̲ your God will restore your fortunes[a] and have compassion on you and gather you again from all the nations where he scattered you. ⁴ Even if you have been banished to the most distant land under the heavens, from there the L̲o̲r̲d̲ your God will gather you and bring you back. ⁵ He will bring you to the land that belonged to your ancestors, and you will take possession of it. He will make you more prosperous and numerous than your ancestors. ⁶ The L̲o̲r̲d̲ your God will circumcise your hearts and the hearts of your descendants, so that you may love him with all your heart and with all your soul, and live. ⁷ The L̲o̲r̲d̲ your God will put all these curses on your enemies who hate and persecute you. ⁸ You will again obey the L̲o̲r̲d̲ and follow all his commands I am giving you today. ⁹ Then the L̲o̲r̲d̲ your God will make you most prosperous in all the work of your hands and in the fruit of your womb, the young of your livestock and the crops of your land. The L̲o̲r̲d̲ will again delight in you and make you prosperous, just as he delighted in your ancestors, ¹⁰ if you obey the L̲o̲r̲d̲ your God and keep his commands and decrees that are written in this Book of the Law and turn to the L̲o̲r̲d̲ your God with all your heart and with all your soul.

The Offer of Life or Death

¹¹ Now what I am commanding you today is not too difficult for you or beyond your reach. ¹² It is not up in heaven, so that you have to ask, "Who will ascend into heaven to get it and proclaim it to us so we may obey it?" ¹³ Nor is it beyond the sea, so that you have to ask, "Who will cross the sea to get it and proclaim it to us so we may obey it?" ¹⁴ No, the word is very near you; it is in your mouth and in your heart so you may obey it.

¹⁵ See, I set before you today life and prosperity, death and destruction. ¹⁶ For I command you today to love the L̲o̲r̲d̲ your God, to walk in obedience to him, and to keep his commands, decrees and laws; then you will live and increase, and the LORD your God will bless you in the land you are entering to possess.

[17] *But if your heart turns away and you are not obedient, and if you are drawn away to bow down to other gods and worship them,* [18] *I declare to you this day that you will certainly be destroyed. You will not live long in the land you are crossing the Jordan to enter and possess.*

[19] *This day I call the heavens and the earth as witnesses against you that I have set before you life and death, blessings and curses. Now choose life, so that you and your children may live* [20] *and that you may love the LORD your God, listen to his voice, and hold fast to him. For the LORD is your life, and he will give you many years in the land he swore to give to your fathers, Abraham, Isaac and Jacob."*

It is simple as that. You want to be revived, then choose life, choose to be positive, choose to love God and others. You have to actively choose to love, and you have to act in love. In Colossians 3:14 we are told to "*put on love.*" We are to be clothed in love. Just like we put on clothes, we need to put on love every day.

Loving Others

I have often wondered why people in general can't seem to get along. Whenever you get more than one person in the mix, there will eventually be conflict. If you look at our advanced world of technological advances, conveniences and access to knowledge, it is amazing to me that world leaders can't get along. There are so many wars; people from different races can't get along, and it is hard to get along with your neighbor next door or the people you work with and a lot of time, unfortunately with those you love- your family. Why is this?

In psychology, there are some answers that have helped me to understand why people can't get along. It labels and describes personality problems as defects, and there can be disorders that cause people to act abnormally in their emotions and behaviors. These personality defects can be fixed and worked on, but the person needs to realize they need help and take action to change the wrong behaviors. Or as the Bible tells us, we have all fallen short, we live in a human body and mind that has been tainted since the beginning. So, every person is defective, and it helps to know and remember that every person sees things a little bit differently than the next. Every one of us has had different things happen to us. We have seen different things, were raised differently, which causes us when we are together to want the other person to do what we expect them to. Jesus calls us to love everyone, even our enemies. Making them our enemy because we don't agree with the way they look at things is extremely wrong. We need to understand where they are coming from, and that God is in control. Our job is not to get them to agree with us, but to be obedient and love them. You can look at people in a different way when you realize we all see things a little differently. Love never fails when it comes to dealing with people; loving our neighbors as ourselves is what God commands us to do.

Being Positive for a Reason

There's nothing like a positive attitude to encourage you, to motivate you, to cheer you up. But just a positive attitude falls short if its motivation is just to be positive and to look good to others. I have seen people like this, who tell everyone to be positive, and if they say anything that they don't condone, then it is negative to them. I have seen people try to be positive, but fail in every area of their life, because it was out of a selfish ambition that motivated them.

There is a positive way to be positive. It is when your positive attitude and outlook and actions are motivated by love, the love of God to be specific. The virtue of love is one that most people strive for in their lives. They seek love; they seek to give love, but a lot of the time we forget why, and a lot of the time we spend on earth is to love ourselves. You see it every day, people that love themselves. They don't get what they want so they take it out on others, or they were never shown love and want others to pay for their pain. So many people are starving for the real love that only comes from God. Real revival can only come when there is real love. Real life is only realized when a life is changed by real love. This is something Christians forget. Sometimes we forget that God has shed abroad His love in our hearts (Romans 5:5 KJV). We are touched by real love and changed, but forget that we are to share that love with others. We should be loving because He first loved us (1 John 4 19). When we start living just for ourselves and our own ambitions, we lose the love that we once had. Jesus warns the church in Ephesus of this in Revelation 2:4 *"Yet I hold this against you: You have forsaken the love you had at first."* How many of us expect God to move powerfully in our lives, but we have forsaken love? We can try to be positive all we want, but without God's love as our motivation, we will fail.

    I want to leave this section with something I wrote from my journal as a young man. The Lord was speaking to me about being positive. It happened while walking home one day in Hanford, California. I took a short cut along railroad tracks to get home. I had just read in the Bible how they made a memorial to God by setting up a pile of stones; you can read the story in Joshua 4 1-9. I was praying about some things and remembering what God had done for me in my life, so while no one was around, I set up a little pile of rocks so that if I went by there again, I would be reminded of what God had done and I did it as a memorial to Him. I knew the rocks would soon be gone, but it was an action that praised Him for what He had done for me, a physical confirmation to Him for what He had done in my heart. As I prayed and dedicated the little pile of rocks to Him, I felt Him speaking to my heart. I was reminded that two negative charges or two positive ones repel, but the negative and positive attract. Here are the thought's/prayer/poem I wrote back on June 6, 1985...

I am not of this world.
As the Rock music blares in the
distance, kids smile with death in
their eyes. The devil's having a hay
day, living it up at the cost of souls.
Children are disappearing, only to be
molested or if they are lucky killed.

*Millions in bondage to alcohol and
drugs. The world is negative; I can no
longer be. I must be positive; I am not
of this world Positive.
Positive is yes, yes Lord I love you.
I will feed your sheep.
I will give up my life to save others.
I must help them change or they will change me.
Cleanse your bride, make her positive and fully
charged or let her realize she already is.
Will we leave this earth and let them die?
Or will we die for them?
Man, from the dust, but in God's image,
precious to the one that made them.*

    We need to positively love everyone, if we don't have love, we have nothing. Everyone needs love and needs to give love. It's the way we were created. The fact that there is love in the world proves to me that there is a God. Think about love for a minute, and read 1 Corinthians chapter 13 in the Bible, then get back to me.

14

FINISH WELL

It seems very easy to start things, but sometimes hard to finish. I have been bad at this in the past, starting things and then losing interest or losing motivation and lack the self-discipline to do the hard work. We cannot do it alone; we need God's strength and motivation to finish. Sometimes it is good not to finish. For instance, if we are trying to do something for our own personal glory instead of doing what God asks us to. Pray about what you are doing in your life and ask God what He wants you to do. He will give you peace and direction if you are sincere, but too often we get lazy; we find other things that interest us more. We get sidetracked. You may have to give up one of or all of your other interests to complete what God has called you to. One thing I know for sure is if you do follow what you know is God's will, you will be happy once you do it. God generally does not have you do things in your life that are against the desires he has placed in you. Our passions and desires are not always the best God has for you. You may be doing something because it is popular or that you have fun doing, or you feel you are good at it, but God may have something you are better at, that truly brings out what your true desires are and you didn't even know it. Jonah was trying to run from God's call to preach to Nineveh, but Jonah thought it was a waste of time. He thought he could predict what would happen, so he thought he would skip it. Once God turned him around, he ended up being instrumental in one of the greatest revivals ever recorded. Do not overlook what God ask you to do, instead, it should be your goal to get done what he asks of you.

Psalm 37:4,5 in the King James Version says:

"Delight thyself also in the Lord: and he shall give thee the desires of thine heart.

Commit thy way unto the Lord; trust also in him; and he shall bring it to pass."

What's Done in the Body

2 Corinthians 5:10 says *"For we must all appear before the judgment seat of Christ, so that each of us may receive what is due us for the things done while in the body, whether good or bad."* This is your only chance. This life is your only life, your only race, your only opportunity to do God's will. It's like a big test. How will you respond? How will you live? What will you do with this life that you've been given? I don't want to see you do bad anymore, I don't want to see anyone be judged for the bad. So why not make something bad into something good? Why not let God revive you and help you?

Today more than ever, people need to see examples of people who are revived, people who are alive in God, not fakes, not people who give up. Anyone can stay depressed or choose to be depressed over failure. Why not choose to be alive again? I know you can do it; I know it is possible. You owe it to God; you owe it to the people in this world. Anyone can live against God; we all have done that. It's time to live for God, to go all out, you will see revival. Un-revived people are everywhere; they have chosen to sit there in defeat, sit there in pain, sit in their failure. There are more than you think who walk around like zombies with no hope, and they don't want to change or know how to change. You have to start, get up, take a step. Your life depends on it! You can be healed, forgiven, revived. Joy can be restored to you, no matter what you have done. You can start by just applying one of these chapters in this book. My prayer is for everyone who reads this to realize they can be revived. My prayer is that you do it now.

Get Up and Finish

In 2008, Heather Dorniden (now Heather Kampf) was running in the final Big Ten 600-meter race in Minneapolis. Two-thirds of the race was done, when she tripped and fell on the track. The other racers ran away toward the final lap, Heather got up in last place and ran like nothing happened. She passed the last girl in third place and continued to move ahead, and at the last second, passed the other two to cross the finish line.

This story and video of the race have inspired thousands. I would encourage you to stop and watch it if you haven't already. Heather said "I always tell people this race isn't just about never giving up; it's about discovering what you're capable of when you are given the opportunity to rise above adversity." Her amazing finish comprised of getting up and finishing. The exact thing you have to do to be revived, to see real change. Maybe you've experienced something a lot worse in life than falling down in a race. Maybe you are dealing with the loss of a job, the loss of a loved one or maybe with the regrets of loss of time that you have wasted. No matter how you feel, even though the feeling can seem paralyzing, you need to get up; you need to get running again, and you need to finish this. Don't let fear hold you down any longer; don't let shame, don't let your circumstances keep you down. Don't let wrong thinking hold you down; break free from saying "I can't," to "I will," and "I can." You can do this. You can get up; you can finish life the way you are supposed to. God will help you. It seemed impossible that Heather could come from last after falling to win the race, but she did, and you can too. If you want to experience real revival, you need to get up and finish.

Quitting is not fun. I have quit things that I thought I had to, and it was never a good memory. In high school I quit cross country because of a physical condition. Later I was able to run again and have enjoyed running through my life. But I wished I did not have to quit that time. There were other situations where I had to quit on my dreams because of circumstances beyond my control, and I felt there was no way out, but did not enjoy quitting. In life, you may have to stop different things for different reasons, but you need to use those experiences as learning opportunities. Most of all, do not use past experiences where you quit or gave up as a deterrent to where you are now and where you are going. God can use those past discouragements to teach you how to overcome bigger challenges and dreams. You must not dwell on the past; you need to learn from the past. If you remain in the state you are in now, will you finish well? What do you need to do to make sure you do not fail in life?

You can change. You do not have to accept mediocracy. You can do it! If you have failed a thousand times, you don't need to keep failing. It's time to do something different. It's time to discipline yourself, it's time to make up your mind that you are not going to end in failure, but that you are going to do what God created you to do- to live and to live abundantly. You have to get up You have the choice to do it or not do it. The choice is yours. Yes, it is hard, life is hard, but you need to condition yourself to get up and run and to keep running. To get out of bed, get yourself ready, exercise. Do what you need to do. Finish what you have left undone, what you know you should do. Quit staying in the comfortable. It's easy to stay on the ground, it takes discipline to get off the ground. Do it, get up, come alive again. Do some or all the things I have talked about in these chapters if that's what you need to do. Train yourself to win. Demand of yourself to get up and win.

"Do you not know that in a race all the runners run, but only one gets the prize? Run in such a way as to get the prize." 1 Corinthians 9:24

The Final Sprint

Most runners tend to train hard so that they can endure at high speeds and have energy to sprint at the end of a race. That final sprint usually determines who will win, if they have anything left. It's called getting your second wind; you get a boost of energy or something inside you pushes in the last seconds to give it all you have. So many people in the race of life do just enough; they run their lives conservatively. They never dig deep to get that last push; they just kind of slow down gradually. Please don't do that. You need to dig down deep with God's strength, and give this life everything you have. You need to get strict with yourself; you need to train in a way to win. You need to train to endure. You need to train so that you can push through the pain and push yourself to sprint to the end. Your life should not be ordinary; it was meant to be extraordinary, to be lived to the fullest, no matter the obstacles you face. Please don't just be average; an average runner doesn't win the race. You need to be above average. Do the unheard of, surprise the spectators. Sprint to the finish and be alive! Whatever you do, do it your best, and give that extra burst. You know the race is short; you know the course will end. Life is like a race, and you only have so long to finish it. Prepare to finish with flying colors. Prepare to hear God say, "Well done, my faithful servant"

I know you can do it. I know you can turn your life around. God has put something special in each one of us. You just need to realize it and do what it takes to share that with the world. I hope that your life will be what God planned for you. Even though you may have suffered loss, I believe in you and know you can change. Say to your bones come alive. Believe you can do it. You can come alive again!

Lately I have been listening in my car to an old song by the Christian band Petra called "Send Revival." The chorus says "Send revival, Start with me." It needs to start with us, with you and me. God gives us free will, and we can choose to be revived or to do our own thing and stay where we are. God will bring revival. He will start with you if you will let Him. He will give you inner revival. So, it is up to you; you have a choice. For your sake and mine and the world's, I hope you choose to be revived.

God Bless you. I love you. Go in peace, and be revived!

www.ingramcontent.com/pod-product-compliance
Lightning Source LLC
Chambersburg PA
CBHW071407290426
44108CB00014B/1725